For Goodness' Sake

Helping Children and Teens Discover Life's Higher Values

A Living Wisdom™ book for parents, teachers, and youth group leaders

For Goodness' Sake

Helping
Children and Teens
Discover Life's
Higher Values

⌒ Michael Nitai Deranja

Crystal Clarity Publishers
Nevada City, California

Copyright © 2004 by Crystal Clarity Publishers
ISBN 1-56589-193-7
Printed in USA

1 3 5 7 9 10 8 6 4 2

Interior Design by Sans Serif Inc.
Cover Design by Lisa Lanthall

Crystal Clarity Publishers
14618 Tyler Foote Road
Nevada City, CA 95959

800.424.1055 or 530.478.7600
fax: 530.478.7610
Clarity@crystalclarity.com
www.crystalclarity.com

Library of Congress Cataloging-in-Publication Data

Deranja, Michael.
For goodness' sake : supporting children and teens in discovering
life's higher values / by Michael Nitai Deranja.
p. cm. — (A Living Wisdom book for parents, teachers, and youth
group leaders)
ISBN 1-56589-193-7 (trade paper)
1. Moral education--United States. 2. Teaching--Moral and ethical
aspects--United States. 3. Parenting--United States. 4. Values--Study
and teaching--United States. I. Title. II. Series.
LC311.D44 2004

2004018084

Contents

From
Indoctrination
to Experience

There is a precious, central strand that runs through all the diverse facets of childhood. Because of its subtlety, this strand can be hard to define, much like the blind men trying to describe the elephant. Some refer to it as moral development, others as spiritual unfoldment, still others as character growth, values clarification, or, as in the title of this book, simply "goodness." This strand, however, is more easily identified if we focus on a few of its key attributes like kindness, cheerfulness, courage, willingness, and self-control. It would be difficult to find anyone who would disagree with the importance of these qualities in a healthy childhood.

It seems exceedingly strange, then, that we find ourselves in the current situation where so many parents and teachers are at a loss when it comes to encouraging values in today's children. How many parents, in the name of open-mindedness, avoid passing on their moral principles to their children? How many schools, citing a fear of lawsuits or a narrow focus on academics, bend over backward to keep from bringing values into the classroom? How did we get to the point where a whole generation of children draws its standards of conduct primarily from television, movies, computer games, and popular music?

While on the surface, goodness may seem to be out of fashion, it takes only a little probing to see that current generations are not really so different from their forebears. Friendship remains one of life's greatest blessings. Truthfulness, however rare its appearance in the mass media, is still deeply appreciated in our interactions with others. Peace, as elusive as ever in the international arena, yet provides a timeless reservoir for personal renewal and well-being. It is not then a shift in our basic values that lies at the heart of our current confusion. What has changed, and radically so, is the context for sharing these ideals with our children.

It was not so long ago that the world consisted of many essentially separate cultures. During those times the question of how to share values with young people was relatively simple to answer. You gathered the children together in the local church, school, or other convenient meeting place and passed on the traditional truths of your society. Because everyone shared the same belief system, there were few, if any, objections, and life rolled along rather smoothly, at least on the surface. But those times are gone. Expanded opportunities for travel and the rise of mass media have brought about an unprecedented mixing of cultures. Societies that were once remote are now part of our everyday lives. Increased levels of interaction, however, inevitably foster comparison and questioning. No longer can educators merely pass on the teachings of a particular religion. No longer can parents assume that their standards are the only ones their children will be exposed to. For better or for worse, the pluralistic society is here to stay.

You may have heard the story of the woman who tried to organize a Christmas party in her office. First there were objections from the Jews about the emphasis on Jesus; then the Muslims pointed out that a party would conflict with their Ramadan fast. After being confronted with the demands for an organic, meat-free alternative from the vegetarians, as well as a seemingly endless array of low-salt, high-fiber, no-cholesterol diets, the woman gave up and took the afternoon off on sick leave.

This woman's approach is mirrored in the reactions of many educators and parents. Faced with the onslaught of differing cultures and belief systems, our tendency has been simply to withdraw from the challenges of character education. Too often we have shown a willingness to settle for the lowest of common denominators, such as zero tolerance for drugs or innocuous discussions on the merits of justice and honesty. Although these approaches may avoid stepping on anyone's toes, they do so at the cost of helping our children become full, dynamic human beings.

Fortunately, we can look at this situation from a more promising perspective. Instead of bemoaning the loss of the "good old days" of simple, homogeneous cultures, we can view the pluralistic society as an opportunity for growth. For if we look more closely at the preceding era, we will begin to notice certain disturbing elements. When everyone belongs to the same church or ethnic group, the unquestioning acceptance of values encourages the thought that "we're right and anyone who believes differently must be wrong." Under these circumstances it is easy to view groups with differing customs as heathens or infidels who are best avoided, proselytized, or, when necessary, massacred. The accompanying self-righteousness and prejudice are responsible for the most sordid chapters in our history books.

A further shortcoming is the tendency to take values for granted. Moral precepts that are authoritatively and rigidly passed down from one generation to another gradually lose their vitality. Succeeding generations may pay lip service to their traditions, but they lack the depth of commitment and creativity necessary for adapting old ideas to the ever-changing demands of contemporary affairs. By contrast, social and cultural interchange forces us to reexamine our values and to realize they are not like stock items that can be stored on a shelf to be taken down on demand. Rather, it becomes apparent that values have real merit only when shared in a living, vibrant manner that reveals their life-enhancing potential.

Early in my life, I had the opportunity to compare the effects produced by two, radically different approaches to moral training. During my eight years at a traditional Catholic elementary school, I was exposed to countless hours of the old-style method of indoctrination, memorizing whole sections of the young people's catechism of beliefs:

(*Question*) Who made us?

(*Answer*) God made us.

(*Question*) Who is God?

(*Answer*) God is the Supreme Being, infinitely perfect who made all things
and keeps them in existence.

(*Question*) Why did God make us?

(*Answer*) God made us to show forth his goodness and share with us his everlasting happiness in heaven.

And on and on . . .

Good grades in religion class could be had by anyone with a well-developed memory. But when it came to more personal issues like the motivation for being good, the bottom line was fear: in the big picture, fear of everlasting hellfire, and in more immediate environs, fear of the nuns' wrath. When I moved on to public high school, I was automatically freed from the lesser wrath. It took a few more years to escape the threat of eternal damnation, but when it did pass, all my formal religious training was swept along with it.

✳

5

There was one incident, however, that produced a more enduring effect. Although I was too young to appreciate all its implications, the freshness and integrity of this event stood out in stark contrast to the other kinds of training I had received. The episode occurred during the winter term of my eighth-grade year, as my friends and I eagerly awaited the end of grammar school. Our sense of anticipation was heightened by heavy rains that made it impossible for us to work off our bubbling adolescent energy on the playground. With no access to a gymnasium, we began to congregate in the boys' bathroom, a place of relative freedom in a school run by women. One day someone suggested we match pennies, a simple game in which two people flip coins, with the winner keeping both pennies. In our advanced state of boredom, this brief taste of gambling caught everyone's imagination. It wasn't long before we were smuggling dice, cards, and poker chips into school. Inevitably, we were discovered and marched to the principal's office. After being chastised for the bad example we were setting for the younger children, we were punished with the loss of two weeks' lunch recess. In a school like ours there wasn't any extra staff, so the person assigned to supervise our punishment was Sister St. John, our classroom teacher. The unfairness of the situation for her was apparent to all of us; because of our misdeeds, she would have to give up her precious midday break. On the day our sentence was to commence, our expectations were for the worst. We all knew she had every right to be upset with us.

I can still picture Sister standing in front of us eight boys at the beginning of that first lunch recess, announcing that we would be spending the next two weeks together. Our imaginations had conjured up all sorts of distasteful consequences: writing "I will not gamble" five thousand times, sitting in silence for two weeks, going without food . . . To our astonishment Sister said that we had the choice of going through two weeks of hell or two weeks of something better. She then handed out copies of a play called "Pitch Black and the Seven Giants." The chance to perform the inverse of "Snow White and the Seven Dwarfs" seemed an appropriate match for our current delinquent status, and we readily chose this alternative. Thus commenced two highly enjoyable weeks of rehearsals, capped by a performance for the rest of our class.

My friends and I were stunned by the whole incident. What had happened to the punishment? The sense of guilt and shame? The scoldings on the evils of gambling? I don't know if Sister really understood all that was taking place, but the end result was that her compassion and goodwill succeeded beautifully in lifting us out of a rather dark and negative state of mind. Later in life I came across a saying that captures the essence of her approach: "You can't drive out the darkness with a stick. What we need is light!" Perhaps she had sensed that our motivations weren't really evil, just an impulsive response to boredom. In fact, with the return of better weather, no one showed the slightest interest in gambling for the remainder of the year.

The experience affected me deeply. I absorbed the seed-thought that there might be more to religion and values than memorizing precepts from a book. Life went on through high school, college, and teacher training, and thirteen short years later I found myself on the other side of the teacher's desk.

As with many teachers, my motivation for entering the profession was to help children become better people. From the start I could see that an exclusive focus on fractions and vocabulary development wasn't going to satisfy me. Students might get high grades in language or math, but could still be insensitive, untruthful, or lacking in courage. What kinds of adults would these children become, and why should I invest so much time and energy for such limited results?

I'd received no help in this area from my education classes at the university where the only reference to values had occurred under the heading of "classroom management," a code word for getting the children to do whatever the teacher wanted. On my own, then, I struggled to address what I came to call the "how-to-live" parts of my children's lives. I began by leading discussions on such values as honesty, kindness, and cooperation. We also read books about people who demonstrated these qualities in their lives. The students were developing a good intellectual understanding of the concepts, but their behavior made it clear that something else was needed before they could integrate these values into everyday life. I had to admit that I wasn't doing much better than the nuns had done with me. And then a second remarkable episode occurred. One morning it snowed . . .

Snow is unusual where I live, and I'd have been a complete ogre not to go along with the children's pleas for a special recess. I stayed inside watching from the window, enjoying the unbounded exuberance of their play. In the space of a few minutes, however, the scene shifted dramatically. First, it was an inadvertent shove that landed someone on the ground, then a wayward snowball hitting another child in the face. Within minutes the whole class seemed to be angry with one another. I rang the bell and called the students in.

After a calming-down period, I asked everyone to join me in the middle of the carpet for a discussion circle. "Can we go outside again?" someone asked. "Only on one condition," I responded, reminding everyone of the topic of cooperation we had been discussing. "Anyone who wants to go out in the snow will have to take a personal pledge to practice the quality of cooperation. The moment you behave otherwise, you'll have to come back in." Everyone, of course, wanted to get back to recess, so we had an impromptu swearing-in ceremony as students solemnly pledged to cooperate with one another. When they returned to the playground, at first there were a few nervous glances in my direction and some overly polite interactions, but gradually everyone settled into good, wholesome, *cooperative* play. Even the architecture was affected. Whereas during the first recess squat, box-like forts seemed to have been the structure of choice, now the children were helping one another create soaring, elegant palaces.

After about half an hour, I signaled for recess to end. We re-formed our discussion circle, and I asked which recess they had enjoyed more. Every hand quickly went up in favor of the second one. When I asked for ideas on why the second recess had worked so well, everyone agreed that the practice of cooperation had made all the difference. If I had any doubts about the power of this incident, they evaporated as I watched the children maintain their cooperation over the ensuing weeks and months.

Here was the alternative I had been searching for to take values instruction beyond the realm of indoctrination. First with Sister St. John I had witnessed the transforming effects of her compassion. Now my students had discovered how the quality of cooperation could make their recesses more enjoyable. Clearly, it was *direct, personal experience* that made it possible for children to appreciate why they should incorporate positive values into daily life.

My challenge, then, has been to explore the possibilities of using an experiential approach to values, one that emphasizes intelligent observation as opposed to unquestioning acceptance. In pursuing this goal, I have had the benefit of a uniquely supportive environment. At the Ananda Living Wisdom School, for more than 30 years there has been a group of parents, as well as a broader community, committed to providing their children with a spiritually inspiring education that avoids the pitfalls of dogmatism and sectarianism. In this laboratory-type situation, I have had many opportunities to experiment with finding ways to share values with elementary students and, in more recent years, with teenagers. In addition, through raising my own son and daughter, I have had the opportunity to apply these insights to the more intimate realm of parenting.

This book presents the fruits of these efforts. In Chapter Two under such headings as peace, trust, and courage, are the games and other activities that have proven helpful in working with children, primarily with 5 through 12-year-olds. Chapter Three shows that these activities can also work with teenagers, but only when integrated into programs that meet their more expansive needs. Chapter four examines such underlying issues as the origins of values and their place in human experience. Chapter five addresses the crucial topic of overcoming restlessness in children and teens, and Chapter six offers suggestions for building healthy adult-child relationships. It is my hope that you will use this book as you would a collection of recipes: useful in getting started, but giving way eventually to your own creative efforts.

2

Sharing
Values with
Children

This chapter presents many games, stories, and other activities useful in sharing values with children. Before jumping into the specifics of these activities, however, it is important to address the overriding issue of tone, or style of presentation. In Western culture, unfortunately, values and morals are often viewed in the same light as castor oil and raw vegetables: good for you, but distasteful. Many of us carry memories of a solemn-faced authority figure lecturing us on the importance of being a "good" person, a term that often carried overtones of sadness and even martyrdom. The underlying message was that we *should* be kind, attentive, and honest even though we'd rather not. This kind of character training is usually pursued with grim resolution, often accompanied by a tendency to keep an eye out for an easier way of getting through life.

The alternative suggested here is based on the observation that positive values actually bring greater happiness and peace into our lives. People who cultivate positive qualities provide bright, attractive role models that are the best possible advertisements for personal growth. The best way to communicate this more cheerful perspective to children is through the language of play. Stories and games naturally convey the essential light-heartedness of qualities like peace, kindness, and trust. With a favorable disposition toward values, children are much more receptive to adult help in cultivating these qualities and in applying them to real-life situations.

The qualities in this chapter are arranged alphabetically, from Attention through Willingness. Suggestions for when and how to use the activities are offered in the chart on the following pages.

The Qualities Chart

Quality	Page #	Suggested Age Range	Suggested Group Size	Level of Use	Story or Incident
Attention	16	4 - 17	1 - 35	Introductory	Yes
Cheerfulness	20	7 - 11	6 - 12	Introductory	Yes
Concentration	23	9 - 17	1 - 35	Introductory	No
Cooperation	25	5 - 17	4 - 50	Both	Yes
Courage	32	All Ages	1+	Established	Yes
Empathy	35	5 - 17	1 - 35	Both	No
Enthusiasm	39	5 - 17	1 - 35	Established	Yes
Friendship	43	5 - 11	5 - 35	Established	Yes
Integrity	46	3 - 8	1 - 35	Established	Yes
Peace	48	7 - 13	8 - 35	Established	No
Self-Awareness	50	7 - 13	1 - 80	Both	Yes
Self-Control	54	5 - 17	1 - 35	Established	Yes
Service	55	4 - 11+	1 - 35	Established	No
Sharing	56	5 - 11	5 - 35	Established	Yes
Trust	58	4 - 17	1 - 35	Both	No
Willingness	61	4 - 17	1 - 50	Established	No
Will Power	64	7 - 17	1 - 35	Established	No

Keys for using the chart

- The suggestions for age range and group size are approximate. Every situation is different, so don't be afraid to try activities outside the guidelines.
- For any group, try to have an age range of no more than three years, unless you can incorporate the older children in helper-type roles.
- By using suggested adaptations found in the text, almost all activities can be used in both small (family) and large (classroom) settings.
- Under Level of Use, "Introductory" refers to a relatively new or superficial relationship between adult and child. "Established" suggests a deeper, more ongoing relationship.

The Quality of Attention

I tell children that we each have hidden muscles. Although we can't see them in the same way as we see our arms or legs, they nonetheless exercise a great influence on us. Memory, reasoning, will power, and attention are a few of the major muscles. If we ignore them, they never develop; but if we exercise them properly, we can strengthen them and greatly improve the quality of our lives.

ACTIVITY: *Attention Trays*

(Age range: 4–17; Group size: 1–35; Level of use: Introductory; Materials needed: tray, cloth, assorted small objects: paperclips, nails, toothpicks, etc.)

Before you meet with the children, arrange several small objects on a tray and cover the tray with a cloth. Have the children gather around the tray so they all have an unobstructed view. Remove the cloth for a few seconds and then quickly replace it. Ask everyone to write down each object they saw.

As with many activities in this book, you can create increasing levels of difficulty. Always begin with a challenge that gives everyone a chance to be successful, for example, five objects displayed 5–10 seconds. You can then build up to 15 objects for 15 seconds, or even beyond. With large groups, an overhead projector will be helpful.

ACTIVITY: *Step-by-Step*

(Age range: 4–17 see note below for younger children; Group size: 1–35; Level of use: Introductory; Materials needed: your list of directions)

Verbally give a complete series of interrelated directions. After a pause of about 10 seconds, ask that the directions be carried out in the exact order you gave them. For example, you could say,

> Draw two large squares next to each other on your paper.
> Place a dot in the center of each square.
> Connect the two dots with a straight line.
> Draw two small circles on the paper, one above the line and the other below it.
> Connect the centers of the two circles with a straight line.
> Draw lines connecting the centers of the circles with the centers of the two squares.

Let children look at one another's drawings or show them a copy of your design. Increase or decrease the number of directions and the length of the waiting period in accordance with your children's abilities.

Adaptation for younger children: Emphasize physical movement as an aid to attentiveness.

> Pick up the eraser.
> Skip across the room and place it on the table.
> Walk around the table three times.
> Pick up the blue book.
> Carry it back to the starting point.

*

Some children will excel at this activity. My advice is to challenge them, letting the others see how far a skill can be developed. To avoid excessive competition, make sure you present a spectrum of activities broad enough so every child can find success doing something. If the competition issue comes up, use it as an opportunity to help children understand that everyone is different, each with his or her special talents. *(Use the following story as an example.)*

STORY: *The Boatman and the Advisor*

In an ancient kingdom there were two boys named John and Philip. Although best friends, they were quite different. John excelled in sports and games; Philip was always the smartest in school. As they grew older, their lives went in different directions. John became chief oarsman on the king's ship; Philip was asked to be one of the king's ministers. One day the king asked Philip to accompany him on a journey to a nearby island. John, noticing his old friend peacefully enjoying the ride while he struggled with his oar, began to be jealous.

When they arrived, the king noticed that John seemed upset and asked what was bothering him. After hearing his explanation, the king paused for a moment and then said, "John, I heard that a litter of kittens was born about a half-mile from here. Would you go and find out how many kittens there are?" Pleased at the chance to prove his worth, John ran off and returned breathlessly in a few minutes with the news that there were five kittens in the litter. The king thanked him and asked, "What color was the mother?" John looked puzzled, but ran off again, to return in a few minutes with the news that the mother was completely black. The king nodded and asked, "What color were the kittens?" For the third time John ran back and forth across the island before reporting that two kittens were black and three were gray.

At this point, with John near exhaustion, Philip asked if he could be of help. The king told him about the new kittens and said he would like to know how many were male and how many were female, but thought it was asking too much to send John again. Philip immediately volunteered. A few minutes later he returned with the information that there were three females and two males. The king glanced at John before turning to Philip. "What kind of place did the mother choose for giving birth?" Philip answered that the kittens were born in a corner of an abandoned shepherd's hut that had a door and two windows, both of which overlooked the north end of the harbor. He said that it looked as though the shepherd planned to return because there was a pile of dry wood next to the stove. The mother had used one of the shepherd's cloaks as a kind of swaddling cloth for her babies, and the cloak's size indicated that the shepherd was quite tall.

The king thanked Philip and sent him away. Turning to John he said, "Now do you see why I rely on Philip so heavily? He is one of the most observant people in my kingdom. No matter what information I need, he either already knows it or can find it out in a fraction of the time it would take others." With that the king walked away, leaving John comforted in the knowledge that Philip's position was not undeserved, but a reward for a valuable skill he had developed.

The Quality of Cheerfulness

Cheerfulness is important for learning how to deal with the ups and downs of life. Sooner or later everyone discovers how things can sometimes start out well, only to go through periods of difficulty. Conversely, difficult situations often turn out to have happy endings. Learning to navigate these fluctuations with cheerfulness is one of life's most helpful skills.

ACTIVITY: *Fortunately/Unfortunately,*
or for younger children use Yeah/Boo (Age range: 7–11; Group size: 6–12; Level of use: Introductory)

Everyone sits in a circle. The leader (probably you) starts a simple story beginning with the word *fortunately.* For example, *"Fortunately,* this morning my father gave me some money so I could buy some ice cream." The next person in the circle continues the story, but begins with the word *unfortunately* and turns the story in a disappointing direction. *"Unfortunately,* the ice cream store was closed today." The next person reverses the tide again and might say, "But *fortunately,* there was a family sitting outside the store making homemade ice cream." The fourth person could add, *"Unfortunately*, the flavor was licorice." The story continues around the circle, alternating positive and negative twists until it gets back to the leader. You can end the story or send it around again, depending on the group's interest and energy level.

STORY: *Everything Turns Out for the Best*

There once was a king who had an advisor known for his unwavering attitude that "Everything always turns out for the best." One day while they were on a hunting trip, the king accidentally cut his thumb so badly that it had to be amputated. As they were returning to the castle, the advisor offered his usual comment that "Everything always turns out for the best." Outraged at the advisor's apparent lack of sympathy, the king had him thrown in the dungeon.

When his wound had healed, the king returned to his favorite hunting grounds. This time, however, he wandered away from his party and fell into the hands of a group of vicious bandits. The bandits believed in making human sacrifices to their gods and were on the verge of making an offering of the king when they noticed his missing thumb. Believing that this deformity made the king impure, they released him and went on their way.

When the king made his way back to the castle, he immediately ran to the dungeon and released his advisor, saying, "Can you ever forgive me? I see now that your advice was correct. My injured thumb actually saved my life." The advisor responded simply, "Yes, your majesty,

✳

as I always say, everything turns out for the best." The king studied his advisor with deepened respect, but then asked, "It may be true that my accident was best for me, but for you it meant an uncomfortable stay in the dungeon. Isn't it true that things turned out badly for you?" The advisor smiled and said, "But, your majesty, if you had not put me in the dungeon, I would have accompanied you on the hunting trip. When the bandits caught us, they would have released you because of your thumb. But as you see, I have no injury that would have kept me from becoming their sacrifice!"

INCIDENT: *Field Trip Frustration:*
A few weeks after introducing this value, my class had the opportunity to test their depth of understanding. We had all been looking forward to an important field trip. The night before our scheduled departure, I found out that our transportation had fallen through and we would have to cancel the trip. As I walked into class the next morning, I was wondering how the students would respond to the unhappy news. To my delight, the entire class took the change of plans in stride, saying that everything would be okay, and that we could now come up with ideas for a new trip.

The Quality of Concentration

What teacher wouldn't want students to concentrate more deeply? Often, though, this quality is worked on only indirectly. I remember reading about a curious educational theory that sought to increase concentration by doing away with the distraction of classroom windows! The following activities offer more refreshing ways of cultivating concentration.

ACTIVITY: *Stretch Your Mind*
(Age range: 9–17; Group size: 1–35; Level of use: Introductory; No preparation)

To expand your children's appreciation for the potential of the human mind, try this activity. Verbally give them a simple three- to five-step mental math problem (e.g. $5 + 1 \times 3 - 4$). (Mathematical purists should momentarily forget about the order of operations rule.) Do something simple enough so everyone can get the correct answer. Next, ask the group to count mentally as you clap your hands rhythmically a few times. Again, everyone should be able to get the right answer. Now, repeat the two kinds of problems, except do them simultaneously. (You may need an assistant to perform one of the tasks.) At first the children will tell you it's impossible to get both answers, but by deepening their concentration, they will succeed.

There is no end to the degree of challenge you can present. Other examples include the following:

Listen to a poem and repeat it verbatim.

Listen to a set of directions for creating a geometric pattern and then produce a sample.

Listen to a conversation and list the topics discussed in their exact order.

Count the revolutions of a wheel that is spinning.

I read about a school that trained its students to do all six activities simultaneously!

ACTIVITY: *Distraction Action*

(Age range: 9–17; Group size: 1–35; Level of use: Introductory; No preparation)

How many times have children told me that they concentrate best with the TV or radio blasting away! Here's a chance to do a little scientific research. Prepare two sheets of math or grammar exercises of similar difficulty. Have the children complete one sheet with the room entirely quiet and the second while there are many loud distractions. (You can bring in a drum, shouting people, etc.) Compare the scores. Be prepared for the possibility that scores may be higher on the sheet done with distractions. The point is not to prove that one way is better than another, but just to show that concentration is one of those invisible muscles that can be strengthened through practice.

The Quality of Cooperation

INCIDENT: *Dog Food Derby*

A group of my seventh and eighth graders experienced the "value" of cooperation in an immediate, tangible way. We had decided to go on a field trip, but needed to earn enough money to make the trip possible. We looked in the newspaper and found an ad for work at a local dog kennel. When we arrived, the owner showed us a huge pile of 30-pound sacks of dog food that needed to be moved across the parking lot into a large shed. He looked a little condescendingly at our group and said he would send two of his employees to help. My students plunged right in, forming a human chain and cheerfully swinging bags down the line. A little later two burly men came out as promised and started working with the kids. After half an hour the men were sweating, panting, and ready for a break. While the men rested, the children continued swinging bags of dog food, finishing the job in half the allotted time. The owner was duly impressed and rewarded their ability to cooperate with a cash bonus.

ACTIVITY: *Cooperate or Die!*

(Age range: 5–17; Group size: 4–35; Level of use: introductory; No preparation)

Find a log (a raised board or even a curb will do) that is long enough to support all your children and ask them to stand on it. To set the scene, tell them that the log is actually a suspension bridge spanning a canyon that is at least a thousand feet deep. To fall off the log is to meet certain death on the jagged rocks below. Now tell them that secret orders have just arrived from headquarters stating that they have lined up the wrong way and that it is imperative they rearrange themselves in a different order (for example, by height or age). Their job is to help one another find their new places without falling into the canyon. Resurrect those who do fall and have them stand next to you to cheer on the others.

ACTIVITY: *Heaven or Hell?*
(Age range 7–17; Group size: 4–50; Level of use: established; Materials needed: two paper plates per child, a roll of masking tape, and one plate of treats for every four children)

Explain to the children that they will be involved in an experiment to determine the difference between heaven and hell. As part of the experiment they will be attending a dinner party that requires special clothes. With the aid of as many helpers as you can gather, tape the paper plates to the inside of the children's elbows so they can't bend their arms.

Have the children sit in groups of four and set one of the plates of treats in the middle of each group. Explain that the etiquette of the meal demands that they not bend their elbows or bring their mouths down to the plates, animal style. You can then lead a short blessing and invite the children to begin the meal. After a few minutes, collect the plates and ask if anyone can explain how the experiment

Students playing Heaven or Hell

shows the differences between heaven and hell. There is a good chance you will get some excellent answers. If the children need more help in understanding the purpose of the activity, you can tell them the following story.

Two groups of people were invited to a very special banquet with dishes filled with all the delicacies anyone could wish for. Just before the first people were led into the room, they were dressed in special dinner coats, quite elegant as the occasion demanded, but cut so that it was impossible to bend their elbows. They were then ushered into the dining hall. To their dismay they quickly discovered that their stiffened arms prevented them from bringing even a morsel to their mouths. Finding it impossible to eat any of the tantalizing food, they all left the room, sure that they had experienced an aspect of hell.

The second group was prepared in the same way as the first, dressed in the strange coats with the straight arms. These people too, were led into the banquet hall and were astonished at the grand display of food. They were seated and, like the first group, quickly realized that their stiffened arms would make it impossible to bring anything up to their mouths. However, rather than feeling downcast at their lot, they discovered that if they focused on feeding one another, they could eat as much as they wanted. At the end of the meal these people left the room, certain they had been given a glimpse of heaven.

ACTIVITY: *Cooperation Squares*

(Age range: 5–17; Group size: 4–50; Level of use: Introductory; Materials needed: file folders or other light cardboard, envelopes, scissors)

Preparation:

- Cut the cardboard into five-inch squares, one square for each child.
- Cut each square into three uniquely shaped pieces, putting the pieces from each square into a separate pile.
- Mix the pieces from four squares together, randomly putting three pieces in each of four envelopes. Clip the envelopes together.
- Continue the process of putting pieces into envelopes until you have an envelope for each child.

Playing the Game:

With the children sitting in prearranged groups of four, place a set of four related envelopes on the table in front of each group. When each child has selected an envelope, ask all the children to remain silent while they reconstruct the four squares by sharing pieces within their group.

Note You can increase the level of difficulty by increasing the number of people (and therefore envelopes and pieces) in each group.

ACTIVITY: *Cooperation Pies*

(Age range: 7–17; Group size: 4–50; Level of use: Introductory; Materials needed: one 8- to 9-inch paper plate for each group, scissors)

Preparation:

- Divide the children into equal-sized groups. For older children and teens, use 3 to 5 groups, with 5 to 7 people in each group. With younger children use fewer children per group.
- In large letters that fill as much of the surface as possible, write one quality on each plate, for example, peace, courage, compassion, forgiveness, charity, patience, perseverance, self-discipline, and joy. With young children you might want to substitute animals for qualities.

- Cut each plate into a unique set of similarly shaped puzzle pieces. To accomplish this task, mark off equal-sized arcs around the outside edge of each plate, matching the number of arcs with the number of members in a group. Place a dot at the center point. Using a distinctive cutting pattern for each plate, cut from each mark on the plate's circumference in to the center dot. For the first plate cut in straight lines, thereby producing pie wedges. With each succeeding plate, choose a different kind of cut (zigzag for plate 2, curved for plate 3, etc.). *See examples below.*
- You should now have one puzzle piece for each child.

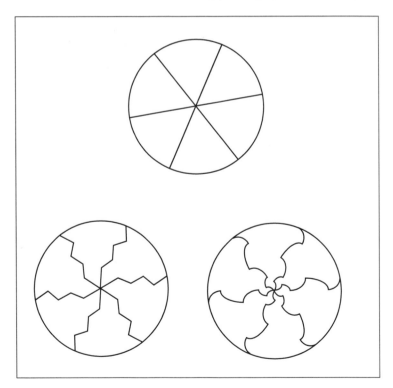

Playing the Game:

Introduce the activity by showing the children a sample whole plate with a word written on it. Emphasize that they will be trying to discover a secret quality and that it's important not to shout out the word when they find it. Tell them that each child will be given one puzzle piece and will need to find everyone else who has a similarly shaped piece. You can mention the total number of pieces that will be needed to recreate each pie, so they know how many children to look for in their group. When they have succeeded in putting the pieces together and know the mystery quality, they should remain quiet and send a spokesperson to let you know they are finished.

Now, shuffle all the pieces together and hand one to each child. Begin the activity with a bell or other starting signal. As each group solves its puzzle, ask that group to sit quietly and wait for everyone to finish.

Alternative Finish: When all the puzzles have been solved, tell each group to spend five minutes creating a pantomime that illustrates their secret quality. Let one group at a time perform their skit. The other children become the audience with the task of guessing each group's mystery quality. Tell the audience that they need to remain quiet during the skit, but can raise their hands as soon as they think they know the answer.

The Quality of Courage

Physical courage can be fostered any time you take children out into nature. You can ask questions such as, Can anyone get on top of this boulder? How high can you climb up this tree? Who can make it to the top of the hill? Challenges of this type are a natural part of a healthy childhood. Moral courage, though more subtle, is also an essential part of a child's growth. Childhood fears come in many forms: fear of the dark, fear of standing up to peer pressure, and, perhaps most important, fear of facing one's shortcomings. The following activity provides an example of how to help children confront these fears.

ACTIVITY: *Slaying the Math Monster [and other despicable demons]*

(Age range: all; Group size: 1 or more; Level of use: Established; No preparation)

In the following example the need for courage is limited to the relatively mundane realm of facing math problems. From an adult perspective, this may not seem particularly significant. In a child's world, however, math offers a simplified instance of the need to respond to all kinds of new experiences: new classmates, new environments, family changes, and more. Learning to respond successfully to these smaller, more confined fears creates a foundation for confronting the larger challenges of life.

A student of mine had a particularly difficult time with new math problems. He did very well when tested on things he already knew, but he would mentally freeze whenever new material was introduced. After helping him painstakingly slog through this quagmire several times, one day I asked if he could see a pattern to his behavior. He said that he could. The next step was to find out if it seemed to be a problem for him. He admitted that it was, not only in math, but also in any circumstance that involved new challenges. I then asked if he wanted to overcome this difficulty. When he agreed, we began to brainstorm solutions. He selected an affirmation he would repeat to himself several times whenever he felt that his fears were getting the best of him: "I welcome everything that comes to me as an opportunity for further growth." My job was to remind him to use his affirmation whenever I noticed that he was beginning to freeze up. As he learned to overcome the difficulty in math, we both saw progress as he applied his new solution-oriented approach to other aspects of his life.

To summarize the process we went through:
1. Identify an unhelpful pattern of behavior.
2. Wait until the child can acknowledge that there is a problem.
3. Make sure he or she is willing to work on it.
4. Brainstorm solutions together.
5. Have the child choose one solution and begin experimenting with it.
6. Find ways to support the child's efforts to resolve the problem.

More ideas for developing courage include the realm of public speaking. When people are asked to rate their greatest fears, dying comes in second to speaking in front of groups. Therefore, it is helpful to provide public speaking opportunities for younger children before the heightened self-consciousness of adolescence sets in. Courage can also be cultivated by getting children to try new things *(see the quality of Will Power on page 64)*.

INCIDENT: *The Wolf of Gubbio*

Everyone reads about courageous acts, but it is difficult to recreate the intensity of the actual event. When working at a summer camp, I decided to use the story of St. Francis and the Wolf of Gubbio. To help the children deepen their appreciation for the depth of faith and courage of this great saint, I asked one of my friends to put on a simple costume and play the part of the wolf. He hid behind a nearby tree while I asked for volunteers for the skit. Quickly several prospective villagers stepped forward as well as three children, aged 7, 8, and 12, who all wanted to play St. Francis. Fortuitously, they lined up by age with the youngest in front.

Soon the villagers were happily going about their daily chores until, suddenly, the wolf appeared. Amidst screams of terror and shouted prayers, the first St. Francis bravely walked up to the wolf and motioned for it to calm down. The wolf, however, had other ideas and let out a ferocious roar. St. Francis whirled around and ran off the stage, much to the merriment of the audience, which included parents as well as other children. The stage was soon reset and the play began again. At the appropriate moment the second St. Francis bravely, if somewhat more tentatively, went forth to tame the wolf. Once again, though, the wolf's savage cries sent St. Francis scurrying for the exit.

Finally, the 12-year-old St. Francis was called. Although the body language conveyed more than a little uneasiness, this time the saint was able to withstand the wolf's cries and gradually calmed it, until it rolled on its back to be petted. St. Francis had risen to the challenge, and everyone had a vivid experience of real courage.

The Quality of Empathy

Awareness of others is the basis for developing empathy. The following activities help children to become attentive, first to others' outward behavior, and then to the more sensitive realm of feelings. Through empathy, children can avoid the pitfalls of prejudice, stereotyping, and unkindness.

ACTIVITY: *Mirroring*
(Age range: 5–17; Group size: 2–34; Level of use: Introductory; No preparation)

In the basic mirroring technique two children face each other with the follower trying to exactly mimic the movements of the leader. Divide the group into pairs, using yourself as the extra person if there is an odd number of children. Let the pairs go off by themselves for a few minutes to decide who will be the follower and who the leader and to practice their roles. Call everyone back and ask each pair to perform in front of the others. Allow about 30 seconds per "act" and then ask the audience to vote on the identities of the leader and the follower. If time and interest allow, repeat the activity by assigning new pairs. This activity also encourages creativity because there are many styles of movement. In fact, after doing this exercise a few times, you can host a talent contest with rewards for most beautiful, unusual, and funny movements.

Students playing Mirroring game

ACTIVITY: *Who's the Leader?*

(Age range: 7–17; Group size: 6–35; Level of use: Introductory, No preparation)

In this exercise 6 to 10 children sit in a circle and choose one child to be the leader. The leader begins a repetitive movement, such as waving the hands, flexing the knees, tapping the head, and so on, with everyone else imitating these movements as closely as possible. While this is going on, another child who has been waiting out of sight and hearing is called into the room and stands in the center of the circle. While the group movement surreptitiously changes every 5–10 seconds, the child in the center has three attempts to identify the leader. For larger groups use more circles, thereby giving more children the chance to play the main roles.

ACTIVITY: *Empathy Chart*

(Age range: 7–17; Group size: 1–35; Level of use: Established; Materials needed: charts)

See Appendix B: Charts, page 140, for the Empathy Chart. To use this chart, copy it on a photocopy machine at 129% increase.

After children have had practice observing and identifying their own feelings (see the quality of Self-Awareness, *see page 50*), use the following chart to develop their awareness of other people's feelings. As with the charts used with other qualities, it's good to have a specified time during the day to fill out the chart. In the left-hand column the children write the names of people they come in contact with daily. In a classroom setting you might need to preselect the names so that everyone is included. At the designated time ask students to color in the blocks next to each name. Choose colors that signify the different kinds of feeling, for example, blue for happy, green for pretty good, yellow for in between, orange for a little upset, and red for sad.

If it seems appropriate, have children compare notes and discuss how they arrived at their choices. Do their observations match people's self-perceptions? If not, what behaviors are being misinterpreted?

For another activity, use the information from these charts for sociological studies. Teach the children how to figure the percentage of time they chose each color for themselves while using the Feelings Charts with the quality of Self-Awareness. Then have them figure the percentage of time they chose the same colors for others on the Empathy Charts. Is there a correlation between how children see themselves and how they see others? For example, when they are sad, do they tend to see others as sad? If necessary, collect the data and share the results anonymously with the group.

Other interesting studies include seeing if there is a critical mass of happy (or sad) people that pull the energies of the whole group up or down? Are some people easier to read than others? Is there a skill to correctly observing others that can be developed through practice?

The Quality of Enthusiasm

A major realization for me as a budding teacher was that behavior is directly related to a person's level of energy. My initial reaction when faced with unwillingness, lack of interest, or just plain boredom was to become upset and proceed as if the children were being naughty. This approach usually succeeded only in making things worse. Eventually, I learned to shift the focus of my efforts to changing my students' level of energy. To my delight, I found that willingness and interest increased dramatically. The following activities have made my life as a teacher much more enjoyable.

ACTIVITY: *Awake and Ready!*
(Age range: 5–17; Group size: 1 to 35; Level of use: Established, No preparation)

This activity attacks the root cause of lethargy by teaching children to use their will power to increase their level of energy. There is even a saying I share with them: "The greater the will, the greater the flow of energy." You will find that these exercises work not only with children, but also are an ideal way to raise *your* energy level whenever you feel tired.

Begin by demonstrating that there are different levels of energy and will. Extend one forearm and tense the muscles, first at a low level, then at a medium level, and finally at a level so high that your arm vibrates with energy. Relax. Now ask everyone to stand and tense a forearm, holding the tension until you have had time to give each child feedback on his or her level of energy. Quickly move from child to child placing your fingers on the forearm and saying low, medium, high, or super-high in response to the level of energy you perceive. Challenge the children to see if there is a limit to the level of tension they can manifest.

Next, introduce the following set of exercises, pointing out that the more energy they put into the movements, the more benefit they will receive from them. At our schools we call these exercises "Superconscious Living" (SCL) exercises, in referring to their effectiveness in raising the level of consciousness. All exercises should be done at a brisk, lively pace.

1. March in place (20-30 times) with arms swinging while repeating aloud, **"I Am Awake and Ready! I Am Awake and Ready! . . ."**

2. Start with the fists touching the chest, then stretch the arms out to the sides while saying loudly, **"I Am Positive!"** Quickly bring the fists back to the chest, then extend the arms forward while saying, **"Energetic!"** Again bring the fists back to the chest, stretch the arms high above the head, open the hands and rise up on the toes while saying, **"Enthusiastic!"** Repeat at least three times.

3. Rub your arms, chest, abdomen, and legs with open hands while repeating several times, **"Awake, Rejoice My Body Cells!"**

4. Rap your knuckles briskly all over your skull while repeating, **"Be Glad My Brain, Be Wise and Strong!"**

5. With closed fists gently but energetically strike the arms, chest, abdomen, and legs repeating, **"I Am Master of My Body, I Am Master of Myself!"**

Students doing Superconscious Living Exercises
showing enthusiasm

After you have introduced the exercises, wait until the group energy is a little low, but not so low that the children are entrenched in negativity. Ask them to notice how they feel, and then have them stand up and do the SCL exercises. Ask if they can notice the change. After the children have experienced the power of these exercises, use them whenever their energy begins to wane.

ACTIVITY: *Raise the Energy*
(Age range: 5–17; Group size: 1 to 35; Level of use: Established)

Whenever the energy starts to drop, look for an antidote. Go outside and run around the building or, if you have to stay inside, do some calisthenics. Bring in some balloons and toss them around the room. Display a large gift-wrapped package in the middle of the room and ask the children to guess the contents. Time the children to see how long they can hold their breath, or keep their arms up, or anything else that is challenging. Lead some rhythmic clapping routines. See if the children can walk while balancing books on their heads, carrying a bell without ringing it, or carrying dried peas on a table knife. Give directions in pig Latin or a foreign language. Practice breathing exercises. See if they can hear a pin drop. Do anything that will take them out of the doldrums. To achieve the best results, begin with a loud, active exercise and then gradually proceed to quieter ones.

INCIDENT: *Catch Me if You Can*

A friend of mine came into his classroom one morning to find everyone drooping with low energy. Not wanting to spend the day wrestling with unwillingness, he stood at the door and called to the children, "The name of the first lesson for today is . . . Catch Me if You Can!" With that he turned and ran out of the classroom. After overcoming their initial state of shock, the children happily raced out the door in pursuit of their teacher. By the time they caught up with him, their lethargy had magically vanished.

The Quality of Friendship

Friendships present some of the most important and chal- lenging learning situations for children. How many times have you seen a child totally devastated by something a friend did? The secret to having good friends, which Dale Carnegie among many others has proclaimed, is illustrated in the following riddle.

STORY: *The Riddle of the Two Dogs*

A dog was roaming the countryside in search of a new home. Coming upon a small village, he trotted up to a farmhouse to see what kind of a reception he would get. Because the front door was wide open, he walked up and cautiously poked his head in. He immediately jumped back in fright at the sight of many growling dogs that began barking furiously. The dog backed away and ran off, convinced that this was a most unfriendly place.

A few minutes later a second dog wandered down the road. He, too, was homeless and went up to the same house to investigate. When he poked his head in the front door, he was delighted to see several dogs, all happily wagging their tales in welcome. The dog knew he had found his next home.

Riddle: How can you explain the completely opposite experiences the two dogs had?

Answer: The house was very unusual in that it was filled with mirrors. The first dog, being suspicious, began to growl at the mirror images. When they growled back, he began to bark. When they barked, he ran off in fear. The second dog was friendlier. His first response to seeing all the dog images was to wag his tail. When they all wagged back, he was sure that he had found a place filled with friends.

The moral of the story: Our initial approach to people largely determines the kind of relationships we will have. Or, as others have phrased it, "To have a friend, first be a friend."

ACTIVITY: *Secret Pals*
(Age range: 5–11; Group size: 5–35; Level of use: Established; No preparation)

From within the group choose an anonymous pal for each child. This can be done randomly or intentionally, but should not be done in pairs because it makes the sharing too personal. Determine the length of the experiment in keeping with the age and interest level of your group. A week is not too long for most children. Pledging everyone to secrecy, let each child know the identity of his or her assigned pal.

At least once each day, every child should do something special for their pal without letting anyone else, except perhaps the teacher, know. Some examples include artwork, inexpensive treats (you may need to put a limit on the money that can be spent), and simple favors like straightening someone's desk or sharpening a pencil. You can provide charts or find another way to remind children to keep their commitments. At the end of the activity let the children guess who has been secretly helping them. Most will have already figured it out, but it's still fun to name people in public. They can also try to remember the special things they noticed.

Ask the children to reflect on the quality of group energy they felt during this activity and then find a way to express this feeling creatively, such as in art, writing, and dance. If the interest level is high, repeat the activity.

As an alternative and more subtle approach, have the children replace the tangible expressions of friendship with intangible ones, like sending good thoughts or simply praying for their pal.

Caution: This activity requires a basic level of trust. If you have children who may abuse it by sending uncomplimentary notes, for example, monitor their actions carefully

✳

so as not to hurt the feelings of others. If you have any doubts in this area, first try the exercises on the quality of Trust described later in this chapter.

The Quality of Integrity

This activity provides a model for indirect intervention in children's lives. It is especially effective when you think a child might become defensive if an issue were addressed directly. Although the listed age range is 3–8, the approach can also be used with older children and even adults (Jesus and his parables, for example) if you are sensitive to the person's level of maturity. The story presented here is also noteworthy for the way it was spontaneously created to meet an immediate situation.

STORY–ACTIVITY: *The Bunny and the Birdie*
(Age range: 3–8; Group size: 1–35; Level of use: Established; No preparation)

A preschool teacher noticed that Sally, one of her younger students, had begun looking up to Mary, an older girl, as a role model. At first the friendship seemed healthy, but gradually Sally began to look to Mary for most of her ideas. One morning the teacher asked Sally if she wanted to play a game. When Sally looked at Mary and asked, "Do we want to?" the teacher changed her plan and called both girls to her side to listen to the following story.

Once there was a bunny and a birdie who were very good friends and liked to do everything together. The only problem was that the bunny always did exactly what the birdie did. If the birdie played in the grass, the bunny would play there, too. If the birdie wanted to rest, so did the bunny. Even when the birdie had worms for lunch, the bunny wanted to eat the same thing.

One day the birdie decided that she was strong enough to fly. She got up on a very large rock and, after a little flapping of her wings, flew into the air. Because the bunny always wanted to do everything the birdie did, she jumped up on the rock, waved her front paws in the air, and jumped. Well, you can imagine what happened. Instead of flying into the air, the bunny tumbled down the steep hill, getting several cuts and bruises along the way. The birdie quickly flew down to help her friend. As soon as the bunny was feeling better, the birdie said, "Bunny, we are very good friends, but we need to remember that we are different. There are some things like flying that I'm good at, and others like hopping that you do well. We'll be best friends if we learn to appreciate our differences as well as the things we can share."

When the teacher finished, Sally looked up at her and said, "That was a *really good* story." The teacher then left, content that she had planted a seed-thought that could be cultivated further when the time was right. Further intervention then would have detracted from the light, playful spirit of the moment.

The Quality of Peace

Peace is a topic very much on people's minds these days. Even with adults there can often be a sense of powerlessness in the face of violent world events. Children, therefore, are even more in need of a way to participate actively in the process of manifesting peace on our planet.

I begin the following activity by starting a conversation on the topic of world peace: "How many of you are in favor of world peace?" Usually, this will include just about everyone. Next I ask, "How many people on the planet do you think would vote the same way?" Again, the answer is almost everyone. The next question is, "Why do we have so many wars if people want peace?" We then talk about how peace happens on three levels: globally, interpersonally, and inwardly. World peace is what everyone talks about and wishes we had, but it can be established only on the foundation of interpersonal peace, a goal much nearer and therefore more immediately engaging for children. When they are faced with the challenge of living peacefully with one another, it quickly becomes apparent that there is yet another level that must first be addressed - the experience of inner peace. How can people live in outward peace if inwardly they are in turmoil? When people are inwardly upset, they can easily misunderstand the motives of others, which, in turn, produces arguments, fighting, and wars.

ACTIVITY: *Peace Pilgrim*

(Age range: 7–13; Group size: 8–35; Level of use: Established; No preparation)

The game focuses on the point that peace is first experienced inwardly. Ask the children if they have met anyone who helped them feel peaceful just by being around that person. Then talk about people whose lifework was to share peace. A woman who took the name of Peace Pilgrim is a good example. In the 1950s she took a vow to walk for peace. Selling all she owned, she began a journey that eventually covered more than 25,000 miles and nearly 30 years until her passing in 1981. Her message was a simple one: "This is the way of peace: Overcome evil with good, falsehood with truth, and hatred with love."

Before the game starts, secretly designate someone as Peace Pilgrim. *(If your group is 15 or more, designate two Peace Pilgrims, thereby quickening the pace of the activity.)* Call the group together and explain that the game consists of everyone walking around the room and greeting one another by looking each child in the eyes, shaking hands, and saying, "Peace be with you." *(You may want to demonstrate this procedure.)* The only exception is that Peace Pilgrim will wink when she or he shakes someone's hand. The person who has been winked at will then greet two more people in the usual way and then sit down in a calm position with closed eyes, exemplifying peace. As Peace Pilgrim completes the journey around the room, more and more people will be quietly seated, and the room will gradually manifest the quality of peace.

I like to close the exercise by sharing the following story from the life of Peace Pilgrim:

I met a couple who were determined that they were going to train their four children in the way of peace. Every night at dinner they gave a regular sermon on peace. But one evening I heard the father scream at the older son. The next evening I heard the older son scream at the younger son in the same tone of voice. What the parents said hadn't made any impression at all—what they *did* was what the children were following. (*Peace Pilgrim: Her Life and Works in Her Own Words,* [Ocean Tree Books, P.O. Box 1295, Santa Fe, NM 87504], page 117)

The Quality of Self-Awareness

INCIDENT: *Boys Will Be Boys*

One day I went into a fifth grade classroom to begin some values work with a group of four boys and six girls. I began the class by saying that we would be doing some special work in the area of feelings and asked if anyone had something they might like to share on the topic. I will never forget the response. Six hands immediately shot up, all waving enthusiastically in the air. The remaining four students had puzzled looks on their faces as if I had just asked the question in Sanskrit or Swahili. As you might have guessed, the waving hands were all from the girls while the puzzled faces belonged to the boys. Although the following activities have been used successfully with both girls and boys, this incident illustrates the special need for helping boys become aware of their feelings.

ACTIVITY: *Body Language*

(Age range: 7–13; Group size: 6–80; Level of use: Introductory; Materials needed: one 3 × 5 card for each student)

This activity introduces several feelings in a fun, nonverbal way. Create a special deck of cards using the following list of traits: kind, cheerful, peaceful, clean, energetic, angry, sad, lazy, worried, and messy. The number of cards will depend on the size of your group, but there should be at least two cards for each trait. The minimum number of children for the activity is 6 (3 traits with 2 cards for each trait), while the maximum is about 80 (10 traits with 8 cards per trait).

Before handing out the cards, tell the children they will need to keep their trait a secret. Give one card to each person and allow a minute of so for everyone to think about how they could express their trait in a non-verbal way. Tell them that they are to observe one another's behavior, searching for people whose actions match theirs. Let the action begin, reminding everyone to be silent. If two children suspect they are expressing the same trait, they show each other their cards. If the cards match, they link arms or join hands and go off in search of other members of their trait family. After a few minutes a few children may seem stranded. Stop the game and ask the "orphans" to demonstrate their qualities for the rest of the group. The appropriate families should then step forward to claim their missing members. When everyone has been matched, end the activity by asking each family to demonstrate its trait and see if the others can guess it.

With younger children introduce this activity in a more concrete way by using animals to represent the different traits, for example: cats for cleanliness, dogs for energy, and deer for peaceful.

ACTIVITY: *Feelings Chart Level One*
(Age range: 7–13; Group size: 1–80; Level of use: Established; Materials needed: charts)

See Appendix B: Charts, page 141, for the Feelings Chart. To use this chart, copy it on a photocopy machine at 129% increase.

Make a copy of the Feelings Chart for each child. In the left-hand column write the times of the day that you want to use for feeling checks. At these times, have the children fill in the appropriate box with such colors as blue for happy, red for sad, and yellow for in between. If there is a request for a wider range of choices, add green for pretty good and orange for a little upset.

This exercise can lead naturally into a discussion of how to change negative feelings into positive ones. For example, is it possible to choose to be happy? Teach the children to practice slow, deep breathing for a minute or two whenever they are beginning to feel upset. If they can catch the mood before it becomes too strong, the results can seem magical.

ACTIVITY: *Feelings Chart Level Two*

(Age range: 7–13; Group size: 1–80; Level of use: Established; Materials needed: charts)

Another, more sophisticated version of the Feeling Chart is described here.

See Appendix B: Charts, page 142, for the Feeling Chart Level 2. To use this chart copy it on a photocopy machine at 129% increase.

Choose a set time each day for filling in this chart.

Check Happy #1 if you are feeling good for no particular reason.

Check Happy #2 if you are happy because something happened that made you feel good.

Check Bored if you aren't feeling much of anything.

Check Sad if something happened that made you feel unhappy.

In the spaces below the chart, answer the appropriate question for each day of the week.

If you checked Happy #1, in what way did you try to share your happiness with others?

If you checked Happy #2, what made you feel good?

If you checked Bored, how did you try to raise your level of energy?

If you checked Sad, what made you feel unhappy?

After the children have had practice observing and identifying their feelings, use the quality of Empathy to help them notice the feelings of others.

The Quality of Self-Control

This quality may seem out of step with the times, when the mass media encourages us to fulfill our every desire and is eager to help us cultivate longings we hadn't even thought of. Nonetheless, self-control can be a tremendous help in learning to overcome life's difficulties. A friend who attended boarding school in England many years ago tells how his discipline problem was handled. He had misbehaved and the headmaster told him that his punishment would be not to go swimming on three occasions when he really wanted to. That was it. No one would check up on him. He was simply expected to follow through on his own. Perhaps this level of self-control is beyond what most of today's teachers can expect, but the incident at least serves as a goal to aspire to.

ACTIVITY: *Gourmet's Nightmare*
(Age range: 5–17; Group size: 1–35; Level of use: Established; Materials needed: food)

Mahatma Gandhi said that self-control begins with the palate. Introduce this activity by sharing stories about people like him who have observed extended fasts or have gone on special diets. Then challenge the children to see how much control they have over their sense of taste. Prepare a "banquet" of typically unpalatable foods, such as cranberry juice, raw onion slices, lime sections, vinegar, ginger root pieces, and cayenne pepper. These suggestions are ranked in my order of offensiveness, but you can alter the arrangement and add other foods.

Divide the children into groups of four to eight. Have one group come up to the banquet at the front of the room, letting each person select a delicacy. When they all have their food, ask them to face the rest of the class and begin eating. The goal is for the children to calmly eat one or more of these foods without showing any signs of disgust. You may have to demonstrate that this task is indeed possible because, as with most character building, nothing can replace a good role model.

ACTIVITY: *Stony Faces*

(Age range: 5–17; Group size: 2–35; Level of use: Established; No preparation)

Divide the group into pairs and have them look into each other's eyes. The first person to smile, laugh, or look away loses. Facial contortions are permitted, but there should be no sounds or hand movements. If you want to bring out the competitive spirit, winners can "face off" against one another with losers doing the same until you have a hierarchy of stony faces.

The Quality of Service

As will be shown in chapter 3, this quality is especially appropriate for teenagers. If children have been introduced to service at a young age, however, it makes life much easier for those who work and live with teens.

ACTIVITY: *Secret Service*
(Age range: 4–11; Group size: 1–35; Level of use: Established; No preparation)

Present the children with the simple saying, "Service Is Joy." Share stories about people such as Mother Teresa who have devoted their lives to serving others, and ask the children why they think people would choose to live in this way. Then give the assignment of testing the saying by doing something special for their families without letting them know what is happening. Examples could include putting newspapers away, sweeping porches, and feeding pets. The next day they will probably be eager to share what happened. Help them find out if their feelings support the saying. If they choose to continue their secret service, ask if they notice any changes in the attitudes of others in their homes.

Note for use with younger children. Consider teaming up a four- or five-year-old with an older person who can help. Make sure the child is involved in choosing and performing the task.

The Quality of Sharing

As with the quality of Empathy story, the following activity is more a description of what can happen when an adult is able to respond creatively to the needs of the moment. The exact mixture of personalities and incidents that determined the conclusion here will never be duplicated. An open and imaginative attitude, however, can produce countless success stories.

INCIDENT/ACTIVITY: *Lunchbox Thefts*
(Age range: 5–11; Group size: 5–35; Level of use: Established; No preparation)

In our school the children bring their lunches from home. One day a girl complained that a favorite treat was missing from her lunchbox. When another student made a similar complaint the following day, everyone began to suspect that someone was stealing food. Quickly the tone of the class deteriorated as children began trying to find out the thief's identity. Because no one would admit taking anything, things were at an impasse until the teacher hit on an unconventional solution. He asked everyone to experiment with bringing an extra treat from home and secretly slipping it into someone else's lunchbox. The next day the tone of the class changed dramatically. Instead of seeing one another as potential thieves, now everyone became a possible benefactor. A few days later the class reflected on what had happened. They all realized that the theft stage produced a tremendous amount of mistrust, whereas the sharing phase produced harmony. The thefts stopped, but the thief's identity was never discovered. More importantly, though, the entire class directly experienced why sharing is preferable to stealing.

The Quality of Trust

My fondest teaching memories are associated with students who demonstrated high levels of trust toward one another. These classes required a minimum of discipline because no one ever intentionally harmed anyone else. Sometimes this quality emanated from a particularly charismatic leader, but at other times it developed gradually through exercises like the ones that follow. Trust and its related quality of honesty provide the foundation for the other values in this book. Until they are established in your group, you will be working against an undercurrent of inharmony.

ACTIVITY: *The Trust Circle*
(Age range: 4–17; Group size: 1–35; Level of use: Introductory, No preparation)
- Divide the children into groups of six to eight.
- Have each group stand, facing one another in a tight circle with one child in the center. For safety's sake, do this activity on a carpet or other soft surface.
- Ask the child in the center to close his or her eyes (blindfolds are another option) and stand perfectly straight, crossing the arms in front of the chest and locking all the joints except the ankles.
- Instruct another child to gently push the center child on the back or arms.
- The children on the opposite side of the circle catch the center child and gently send him or her back.

If the child in the center succeeds in locking the hips, knees, and shoulders, the feet will stay in one place while the rest of the body pivots around the circle, completely at the mercy of the other children. After a minute or so, have someone else take the center spot, continuing until everyone has had a turn.

Students playing the Trust Circle game

Note for families and younger children. Instead of a group circle, simply stand directly behind the child. Ask him or her to close the eyes and lock the joints as in the group activity, and then let the child fall directly backward into your waiting arms. You can stand as close as is necessary for the first attempt and then move gradually apart as the trust level increases.

ACTIVITY: *Trust from Above*
(Age range: 9–17; Group size: 8–35; Level of use: Established, No preparation)

If you have a particularly trusting group, try a version of this game that my fourth and fifth grade discovered while on a camping trip. We gathered around a large tree stump about two feet high. The students took turns standing blindfolded on the stump with all limbs locked as described in the Trust Circle, and then falling backward into the arms of the rest of us who were standing on the ground. It was a big challenge for the blindfolded children not to protect themselves by bending their knees or reaching with their arms, but after a few attempts everyone succeeded. Be prepared for the moment when the group turns to you and asks if *you* trust them. I still remember the sensation of letting my six-foot 165-pound body fall into space, hoping that my group of four-and-a-half-foot tall, 90-pound students were up to the task! Fortunately, they were.

ACTIVITY: *The Trust Walk*

(Age range: 4–17; Group size: 1–35; Level of use: Introductory; Materials needed: blindfolds for half the group)

For this popular activity, pair the children and have one member of each pair put on a blindfold. The "seeing" child grasps his or her partner by the hand and elbow simultaneously and walks carefully around the area you have chosen. Ahead of time point out such hazards as low tree limbs or steps, and intervene quickly if anyone seems tempted to run or otherwise jeopardize his or her partner's safety. After two or three minutes, everyone reverses roles. The children will often want to retrace their routes with eyes open.

The Quality of Willingness

Gather the children and lead a discussion on how willingness differs from unwillingness. Through role-playing they can model varying approaches to such tasks as cleaning their rooms, washing dishes, and doing homework. Draw out the children's observations, highlighting such insights as willingness makes us feel better, gets things done more quickly, encourages creativity, and in general is just more fun. Supplement the discussion with stories that emphasize the benefits of willingness.

ACTIVITY: *Willing or Unwilling?*

(Age range: 4–17; Group size: 1–50; Level of Use: Established; Preparation: jobs for everyone)

The Preliminaries. Set aside 10–15 minutes each day for classroom or household cleanup and related chores. Divide the children into groups and assign jobs. For variety, rotate the chores daily but keep the children in the same groups for the duration of this activity.

Practicing Willingness. Begin each cleanup period with a short meeting in which the entire group agrees on a particular approach or attitude that will be used as a means of practicing willingness. Examples include:

1. Offering verbal encouragement to one another such as "Good job," and "Way to go!"
2. Listening to rousing music or singing an appropriate song while doing their tasks
3. Starting with the Awake and Ready Exercises (see the quality of Enthusiasm, see page 39)
4. Repeating an affirmation such as "Energy and joy flow through my body" while they work (You might also have the children close their eyes and visualize this energy flowing through them.)
5. Keeping their minds focused on positive thoughts such as "See how much we're getting done," or "It feels good to get everything clean."

The Experiment. After three to five days, while the energy for this activity is still high, call for an experiment with unwillingness.

- Have each group choose one of the positive approaches they've used and practice it for the beginning of today's work period.
- Tell them that after three minutes you will ring a bell, at which point they are to switch to a negative, complaining style of behavior.
- Ringing the bell a second time will be their signal to switch back to a more positive approach. The length of the negativity period should be long enough for them to experience the shift of energy, but not so long that they lose the ability to switch back!
- Close the experiment with time to introspect and share (verbally and/or in writing) their experience of the differences between willingness and unwillingness.

ACTIVITY: *Testing the Opposites*

If the above experiment goes well, help the group choose a different pair of opposite qualities to investigate. Possibilities include kind vs. mean, calm vs. worried, clean vs. messy, happy vs. sad, and honest vs. dishonest. Design similar methods that give the children a chance to experience the effects of the different qualities. Help them to record their feelings throughout the experiment.

The Quality of Will Power

Sometimes children can surprise us with completely unexpected levels of will power, perhaps because they don't know what their limits are supposed to be. Once I was working with two nine-year-old girls who were preparing to pass a swimming competency test. Among the required skills was the ability to tread water for 10 minutes. The girls had asked me to time them as they practiced. Five minutes passed, then ten, with neither girl wanting to be the first to stop. Fifteen, twenty, then thirty minutes went by as the girls challenged each other to keep going. Finally, after 60 minutes of nonstop effort, they both hopped out of the pool, happy and only a little tired from their exertions.

ACTIVITY: *Five Kinds of Will*
(Age range: 7–17; Group size: 5–35; Level of use: Established; No preparation)

Will power is among the most important of the invisible muscles of character development. Because of its invisibility, however, it is hard for young children to grasp its value as well as the subtleties of its use. A helpful approach is to involve children in a role-playing activity that highlights the following five stages of will power:

Stage One: Physiological Will: An instinctive urge to satisfy basic physical needs such as hunger, thirst, and the avoidance of pain. Babies are the clearest example of this kind of will.

Stage Two: Unthinking Will: The passive acceptance of other people's ideas or commands that young children often show toward their parents.

Stage Three: Blind Will: The careless exercise of newly awakened independence or rebellion that is common among older children when they act without concern for the consequences.

Stage Four: Thinking Will: The need to consider the probable effects of one's actions and choose those actions that promise beneficial results. Usually develops out of the catastrophes of Stage Three.

Stage Five: Dynamic Will: A highly refined development of the will that is best demonstrated by the lives of people like Lincoln, Gandhi, and Mother Teresa. This stage reaches for a goal that seems impossible to most people, and then succeeds because the person is able to draw on seemingly superhuman sources of energy.

After describing these levels, divide the children into groups of five. Tell them to decide among their group who will portray each of the five levels. When the casting is complete, ask each group to choose a dramatic setting, for example, climbing a mountain, rowing a boat, making dinner, or other group endeavor. If there are difficulties in choosing parts or selecting plots, provide help as needed. Give the groups 5–10 minutes to practice their skits, then call all the children together. Tell them that as each group performs, the job of the audience is to decide which character is portraying which level of will power. Make sure the audience lets each group play out its skit without interruption. Children can raise their hands when they think they have figured out the characters, but must wait for your signal before voicing their ideas. If the acting seems vague, ask for volunteers from the audience to demonstrate how the different levels of will might be portrayed.

ACTIVITY: *Strengthen Your Will*

(Age range: 7–17; Group size: 1–35; Level of use: Established; Materials needed: charts)

Begin by introducing three ways to strengthen the will.

1. Do one thing at a time.
2. Finish what you start.
3. Try one new thing a day (something you've never done before).

Then give each child the Will Power Chart to help them develop their will power.

See Appendix B: Charts, page 143, for the Will Power Chart. To use this chart, copy it on a photocopy machine at 129% increase.

Each day have the children check the appropriate box if they accomplished any of the goals. (They can make multiple checks if they did more than one new thing, finished several tasks, etc.) Ask them to briefly describe what they did on the lines below the chart.

Countless stories illustrate what people have been able to accomplish through a determined application of will power. An interesting sidelight is to present examples from history that show how the development of will power without a balanced cultivation of sensitivity and intelligence can lead to fanaticism and cruelty (Hitler, Stalin, the Spanish Inquisition, etc.).

3

Sharing
Values with
Teens

The experiential approach to val-
ues described in chapter two provides a firm foundation for
moral development. As a result, it has been my delight over
the years to spend time with many sensitive, enthusiastic
children. However, as the humorist P.G. Wodehouse wrote,
"There is always a fly in the ointment, a caterpillar in the
salad." In our school the caterpillar was puberty.

As the children reached the teenage years, it became clear
that our program needed further refinements to successfully
meet their changing needs. Yes, they still had their basic
qualities of integrity, cooperation, and other aspects of good
character, but this foundation was becoming overgrown

with weeds of restlessness and boredom. Other warning signs included a preoccupation with fads and material possessions, an absorption with personal problems, a growing aloofness from adults and disdain toward younger children, and subtle rivalries that found expression through put-downs and other insensitive remarks directed at one another. Were these symptoms, as some suggested, just the standard characteristics of adolescence? Our success with younger children encouraged us to seek a solution.

Adventures in Mexico

These issues came into sharp focus one autumn while I was working with a group of 7th and 8th graders.

Looking for some way to shake the class out of their lethargy, I began talking with Ofelia Sanchez, the mother of one of our teachers, who was paying a short visit to our school. When she asked how things were going, I told her of my search for a new kind of experience for the older students. Ms. Sanchez, who had grown up in Mexico, became excited as she told me how she was still in close contact with the people there, in particular a Padre Fernando, the priest in charge of an orphanage in La Paz. She thought he would welcome a visit from a group of American teenagers. I was immediately intrigued by the idea and began investigating what it would take to transport, house, and feed my students during a two-and-half-week trip to Mexico.

Being fairly ignorant of Mexican geography, I was hoping that La Paz would be close to San Diego, a relatively inexpensive destination. But no, La Paz is situated at the furthest tip of Baja California. This first hurdle was cleared, though, with the help of some friendly people at Aero California who offered us an affordable group air fare when they found out why we were traveling. Another unexpected blessing occurred when Padre Fernando invited us to stay in the orphanage, thus greatly reducing our food and lodging costs. Still, the price per person for the trip came to $400. Ms. Sanchez's daughter, Irene, suggested we ask each of the students to raise half of the money, with parents putting up the rest. In this way the students could share in the experience of manifesting the trip.

Our presentation to the children caught their attention, and we fixed our departure date for the following spring. It wasn't the easiest winter of my teaching career, but the goal of visiting Mexico kept everyone moving forward. Under Irene's direction most of the students earned their money by helping out at the local thrift shop. Car washes, firewood-stacking, and other odd jobs also helped. We made use of class time to study Spanish and Mexican culture.

At last the long-awaited day came. After many hours of train and plane travel, we arrived at Ciudad de los Niños y Niñas, the orphanage in La Paz where we were to spend the next two weeks. Padre Fernando and some of his older boys picked us up at the airport in an old school bus. My students were mesmerized by the sights as we traveled across town and finally through a large metal gate that led into an open courtyard. There, waiting for us, were about one hundred Mexican children between the ages of 6 and 18. Even as we descended from the bus, the friendships began with the children offering to carry my students' luggage. We were quickly settled into the boys' and girls' dorms.

Thus commenced two weeks of intensive cultural exchange. There were so many differences. First there was the lifestyle without parents. Four nuns and two priests supervised the entire orphanage, a ratio of about 16 children to one adult. Then there was the food. At dinner the night of our arrival, we were served tortillas, beans, and rice, with milk that we heard had been specially donated in honor of the Americanos' visit. We were surprised the next morning when the same items were served for breakfast, but after a similar menu at lunch, we realized that this was the standard diet. Interestingly, toward the end of our stay we decided to offer a little variety by providing pizzas for dinner. The children politely accepted our offering, but then asked if there couldn't also be tortillas, rice, and beans!

We noticed a similar pattern with the clothing. On our second day we saw many of the same shirts and pants on the playground that we had seen on the first day, but this time on different bodies. A little detective work revealed that the children didn't have personal wardrobes, but shared from a common closet. From this observation we discovered that the children also lacked many of the other "necessities" of American youth: no Walkmans, CDs, or other electronic gadgetry so important to my class. In fact, we discovered that each child had a small box—about 6 inches high by 15 inches wide by 10 inches deep—which contained all personal belongings.

Then there was the matter of washing clothes. The two old machines were reserved for sheets and other communal items. Personal laundry was done in large basins on a washboard—by the girls! Needless to say, reactions to this division of labor were polarized. Everyone, though, pitched in for cleaning. We got up at 5:30 each morning to help sweep and mop every square inch of the dormitories and patios, and then continued with breakfast prep and dining room set up. Games were simple, using such "toys" as bottle caps and sticks. We introduced the children to ping-pong by stringing a net we had brought across a dining room table.

One highlight was getting to know Moses, a year-old boy who was dropped off at the orphanage by a woman who assured everyone that she would return in "just a few minutes." We learned that almost all the children had at least a relative or two, but that people simply didn't have enough money to care for them. Staying at the orphanage was voluntary, but the alternative for most children was living on the streets, an option that resulted in a considerably shortened life expectancy.

Over the next two weeks friendships blossomed in spite of the language barrier with much trading of pictures and other handmade gifts. As the shock of cultural differences wore off, my students began to notice that for all their simplicity—some would call it poverty—the children were quite happy. From my perspective, they seemed even happier than their more materially affluent American counterparts. What a mystery!

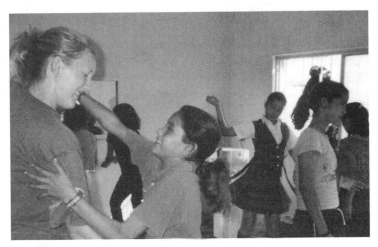

Students dancing

Students developing lasting relationships

When our stay was finished, there were many tears on both sides. Some of my students' thoughts are expressed in the following excerpts from papers they wrote at the end of the trip.

Student #1 "When I first thought about orphans, I thought of sad, bedraggled little kids. Now after spending two weeks in the Baja orphanage, I have to admit I almost wished I was one too. They were so happy and carefree. I live so well, I have tons of things they can only dream of having . . . and yet when I was there, those were some of the happiest days of my life. The trip was such an opening experience for me. I learned how to live with a lot less and to enjoy and live in each moment. I learned to share what I have, and to accept it when I don't get what I want. I learned also to be kind to every one. For me, living in an orphanage was wonderful!!!"

Student #2: "I learned to be grateful for what I have and to not judge ANYONE before I know them. It was hard at times having to face ants and the same food everyday, but there were always good things to overcome the bad ones, like their kindness, the gifts they gave us, and the precious moments we shared."

Student #3: "I learned to miss my parents. I know it sounds weird, but when we were there I realized that most of the children don't have parents to miss. And I realized that missing my parents is not a bad thing. It makes it real to say 'I love you.'"

＊

Student #4: "Mexico and the United States both have people who love and hate, people who are good and bad, people who are rich and poor and even homeless. People in Mexico may look different, act different, have different customs and speak a different language, but in our hearts we're all the same no matter where we live. All people sometimes feel joy, happiness, excitement, embarrassment, sadness, confusion, regret, anger, shame and guilt. We are all trying to live in a hard world struggling to deal with confusing and complicated feelings."

The visit to Mexico marked a turning point in the development of our school and in my own understanding of adolescence. To begin with, there was the striking fact of the trip's success. When we returned, my students had changed in significant and lasting ways. They were more accepting of younger children, more open to adults, and less competitive with one another. For a short time they even continued to get up at an early hour and look for ways to help out around their homes. The trip had satisfied an important need that allowed their better qualities to shine forth again. With the haze of discontent lifted, here again were the young people I had watched grow up as cheerful, exuberant children. (And who later matured into thoughtful, responsible young adults).

It became clear that many of the earlier behavior problems in this group could be traced to a lack of compatibility between their changing needs and the program they were being offered. During childhood, the job of parents and teachers is to create a kind of garden (the word *kindergarten* comes to mind), a miniworld that is colorful, harmonious, enjoyable, and protected from the potentially harmful aspects of life. However, with puberty children begin to outgrow this sheltered refuge. They require a more challenging and expansive experience, a bridge of sorts toward the diverse conditions of the broader world. The program in our school, like that of so many middle and high schools, was far too similar to what we had offered when they were younger. Yes, there were advanced math classes and more difficult history courses, but everything was still second hand, once removed. What the Mexico experience provided was a taste of real life, with real people and real challenges.

An interesting story illustrates this point. A group of students had engaged in a study of the life cycle of butterflies. One of the first things everyone noticed was how difficult it was for the caterpillars to force their way out of their cocoons. With the idea of helping, the students very carefully cut the cocoons so that the caterpillars would have an easier time. To their dismay, the students saw that when the caterpillars grew into butterflies, their wings were too weak to allow them to fly. It was only then that the class realized that the effort involved in extracting themselves from their cocoons was an essential part of preparing the caterpillars for the butterfly stage.

Similarly, through blindness or a misguided notion of love, adults sometimes try to shield teenagers from the more formidable aspects of the world: the need to earn money, for example, or such problems as war, prejudice, hunger, and pollution. However, it is through involvement in just these challenges that teenagers build the responsibility, courage, and self-confidence that helps them become effective adults.

From my observation, there is a window of idealism that occurs between the ages of 12 and 14. When teachers and parents provide opportunities for constructive engagement in meeting life's challenges, the exuberance of childhood can evolve into an enthusiastic adolescence. If these opportunities are lacking, the earlier brightness tends to dim into self-absorption, boredom, and rebellion. The need for an expanded experience of life is simply a fact of adolescence. When our society and our schools ignore or even resist this need, teens will fulfill it by whatever means are available. All too often this quest for new experience leads to sex, alcohol, and drugs.

Student with "Moses" during trip to
orphanage in La Paz, Mexico

From this point on, service adventures, as we began to call them, became the focal point of our 7th to 12th grade program. Often the trips provided a dynamic motivation and rationale for other aspects of the curriculum: foreign language study, comparative cultures, and history, for example. There have been several more trips to Mexico, returning to La Paz and then on to other orphanages in Las Mochis and Mazatlan. In addition to renewing friendships, we created a new mural each year on one of the orphanage walls to commemorate our visits. Once we traveled down the Baja peninsula by bus to get a broader experience of Mexican life. We participated in oceanography classes at

Students helping with sea turtle research

a college in Ensenada, waited on our bus for several hours while a flash flood receded from the highway, and rowed out on a quiet bay at sunrise to watch whales. The students even developed a special classification for Mexican hotels: Hotel 6 was akin to the lower end of American motels, Hotel 3 meant they felt safe going barefoot in the room, and Hotel minus 2, meant they were afraid to sleep between the sheets.

Adventures in Italy and India

It has been amazing to see how wide the doors to adventure have flung open at our quiet knock. On two different occasions we were able to go to Italy, and once all the way to India. For our first Italy trip I had been unable to arrange a service project via my phone calls from California. Determined that we have more than a tourist excursion, I began looking for possibilities immediately after our arrival. A woman told me about a camp for people fleeing the war in Kosovo that was being set up in a town just 15 miles from where we were staying. Two days later my students, all 15-17-year-old-girls on this trip, were serving as hostesses for about 150 refugees. Surprisingly, many of the Kosovars spoke English, but no Italian. As a result my students became the primary communicators with these people. As we sat for dinner the first evening, the refugees told us about some of their terrible experiences. My students listened intently as one man told us how all Serbs (their enemies) were devils and needed to be massacred. His friend sitting next to him, though, disagreed and said that the Serbs had just been listening to the wrong person (their dictator, Milosevic) and needed to be helped to see a better perspective on life. Then it would be possible to learn to live together peacefully. Thus, my students heard two views that offered widely divergent pathways for the future of this war-torn area. This experience also showed us that we could help with the big problems that land on the front pages of the newspapers as well as with the seemingly smaller ones we were usually involved with.

Later during the trip my students were walking ahead of me as we explored the streets of Assisi. As I caught up with the girls, I found them happily interacting with a group of elderly people. It turned out that they had stumbled upon the local *Casa di Riposa*, the Italian version of a retirement home. There was much laughter and many smiles in both groups as they tried to communicate and in some cases even sing. Language, age, and cultural barriers succumbed easily to the girls' outpouring of warmth and enthusiasm. On our subsequent trip we built on this initial interaction through regular visits to these elderly Italians. Through songs, smiles, and gradually improving Italian, we participated in a weekly exchange of energy that consistently uplifted everyone's spirits.

In India I watched one of my students create a friendship with a beggar afflicted with a terrible disease that left the right side of her otherwise attractive face completely disfigured. Here was the ability to look beneath surface appearances to touch the underlying humanity. While we were at the Mumbai (Bombay) Airport preparing to depart, I needed to make some travel arrangements and left the

Indian friend of one of my students

girls in the parking lot for a few minutes. The area was dirty, full of pollution-producing taxis and buses, and a major congregating place for beggars—in short, not a particularly uplifting environment. When I returned about 10 minutes later, I witnessed an unexpected sight: in the middle of the lot, my girls had joined hands with several of the girl beggars and were teaching them a circle game. All were laughing and thoroughly enjoying one another's company, though they couldn't communicate verbally. Taxi drivers, adult beggars, and passers-by all watched the girls, visibly touched by their joy. The girls had learned how to transform an unpleasant experience into a positive one by expressing kindness, high energy, and cheerfulness. Once again cultural, economic, and social barriers had disappeared.

Adventures Closer to Home

Of course all of our experiences weren't so exotic, and as the value of service adventures became clearer to the students, we were able to engage in projects closer to home. We found an inspiring homeless shelter in San Francisco called Martin de Porres, named after a Catholic saint who helped many impoverished people. The volunteers welcomed our help and even opened up the staff residence as a place for us to stay. As we got out of our van for our first overnight visit, we witnessed a drug bust going on across the street. "PUT YOUR HANDS UP AGAINST THE WALL!!!" the police yelled through a bullhorn. In response to our somewhat shocked expressions, our hosts commented, "Oh don't mind them, it happens around here all the time." At the shelter we were able to interact with the truly homeless, the people who sleep under cardboard or newspaper on the sidewalks. I was impressed at how easily my students got into the flow of serving soup, cleaning tables, and talking with the shelter's guests. We encountered all kinds of people, from the obviously destitute to the man in a business suit who came in and filled up his rather large briefcase with containers of soup. We talked with one woman who had become homeless after being robbed of all of her possessions. Now she was hesitant to return to a more normal lifestyle, saying that she had never before felt so close to God.

In the National Parks we discovered a program called Volunteers in Parks where we could work in exchange for the usual entrance and camping fees. After performing our service project, we always had plenty of time for hiking and exploring. In this way we could experience the incredible beauty of the waterfalls, gorges, and other sites, along with the satisfaction of doing something tangible to maintain these amazing places. Through this program we have painted garbage cans in Yosemite, helped with plant restoration on the rim of the Grand Canyon, maintained trails at Mesa Verde, and picked up large quantities of litter from Bryce Canyon in Utah to Angel Island in San Francisco Bay.

Students during service project on the rim of the Grand Canyon

For the past several years we have incorporated service projects into our regular weekly class schedule. At first it was difficult to find local agencies willing to accept teenage volunteers. We did find a program, however, that was desperate for help—a daycare center for people suffering from Alzheimer's and other forms of dementia. I was impressed at my students' patience with people who are among the hardest to serve. For example, during a simple game of cards the rules would have to be explained for every turn. The students did such a good job at the center that they won a countywide award that year from the JC Penney Company.

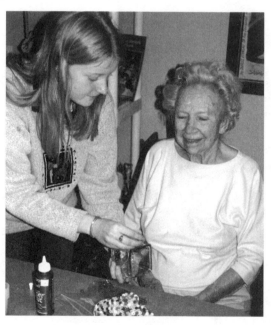

Student helping with craft class
for Alzheimer's patients

Gradually other doors opened. We began helping at the Interfaith Food Ministry, a local food bank. Here volunteers from many local churches gather, package, and give away food donated by various businesses. At the local animal shelter we cleaned and exercised dogs and cats to give them a better chance of being adopted. We began working with an inspiring group of teachers who help severely handicapped children in our area. Charlie Brown, a woman who specializes in working with Downs syndrome patients, said that when she started her career, the average life span for people with this handicap was around 25 years. In that era they were placed in institutions where their only recreation was to sit all day in front of a TV in a large, drab, pale green room. As ways have been found to involve them in a wider range of activities, their life span has lengthened to the point where it is now similar to that of the normal population.

Student playing chess in a retirement home

Other activities have included providing child care at a local shelter for homeless mothers so the moms could have a chance to work on other aspects of their lives. When a forest fire broke out about 25 miles north of us, we spent the day working with children from that area, helping them draw pictures, write stories, and just talk about their traumatic experiences. Some students, inspired by their involvement in service, created a play about Mother Teresa and performed it in several local schools. A particularly poignant service opportunity occurred in the large home that serves as a dormitory for the girls in our boarding school. A man and his mother had moved into the house to help in various ways. Soon after the start of the school year Evelyn, the mother, was diagnosed with a terminal illness. Over the next few months, as she weakened, the girls took over more and more of the nursing duties. Their reward was even more apparent than usual as they gained access to the fruits of Evelyn's many years of wise living. Her motto, which she practiced up through her final hours, was pinned to her closet door: It read: Happiness is a choice.

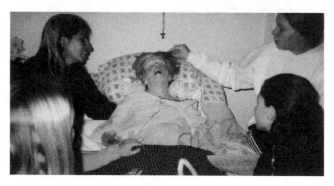

Teacher and student attending to Evelyn's last needs

Guidelines for Service Adventures

If you feel drawn to work with teens, here are some guidelines for setting up service adventures.

1. Choose an appealing first activity, particularly if the concept of service is unfamiliar to your teenagers. To overcome aversion to new ideas, especially those proposed by adults, select something exotic. Teens are unlikely to turn down the opportunity to travel. Gradually they will appreciate the subtler rewards of service.

2. If you travel, make sure there is involvement for them and not just entertainment. Most teenagers make poor tourists, at least in terms of appreciating history, architecture, or music. Find ways to get involved in hands-on projects that can activate their interest and enthusiasm.

3. Find the right balance of service and fun. Our work at the orphanage was interspersed with visits to the incredible Baja beaches. One unexpected experience involved the nuns from the orphanage joining us in swimming, stylishly outfitted in their flowing black robes!

4. Involve teens in raising money for the trip. If nothing else, this requirement will filter out the unmotivated people who would drag down the energy for everyone else. This step also helps teenagers realize that they have the power to make things happen simply by focusing their wills.

5. Be prepared to deal with negative teen stereotypes when you seek out prospective service projects. Opening their doors to an energetic group of young people may not be high on some people's to do list. If you find this to be true, try looking for those areas of service that no one else is interested in (as with the Alzheimer's patients above).

6. Emphasize interactions with people. Although painting playground equipment and picking up litter are worthy forms of service, I've found that working directly with other people is generally more satisfying to teens.

7. When you set up a longer-term program, try to offer a choice of service projects. Everyone has preferences, and acknowledging them helps keep the energy high.

4

Values:
Sectarian or
Universal?

We have explored some of the exciting opportunities presented by an experiential approach to values. Now it is time to take a fresh look at the greatest obstacle to implementing programs of this kind in our schools: the issue of church-state separation. If, as some believe, values are sectarian, then in a pluralistic society it is clearly unjust to impose one set of values, and, therefore, one religion, on everyone.

This issue is related to the topic of indoctrination discussed in the opening chapter and affects our basic understanding of values. As was pointed out, societies of the past have been mostly homogeneous, with one primary culture and one dominant church. Because churches were the primary custodians of morality, people began to think that values were somehow created or owned by their particular religion. Thus, we have such terms as "Christian humility" and "Buddhist compassion." This kind of sectarian bias, however, has become increasingly difficult to maintain in our present era of cultural diversity. Today, it is relatively easy to observe compassion or humility being expressed by Moslems, Hindus, and even atheists, just as it is possible to find instances of pride and insensitivity in Christians and Buddhists. These observations suggest that no one religion holds a monopoly on virtue. A brief review of the world's primary scriptures offers additional support for this view. In spite of the well-known hazards of quoting sacred writ, I have included a few passages at the end of this chapter because they illustrate so clearly how religions all embrace the same basic values. The essential point, then, is to place our focus directly on the values themselves instead of on their often-conflicting religious presentations. In this way we open the doorway to bringing values instruction back into the classroom.

The universal nature of values is readily apparent in the way they permeate our lives. How can anyone overcome difficulties on the job without perseverance? How can parents respond effectively to the needs of their children without empathy? How can a person stay out of debt without self-discipline? The list could go on and on until it becomes apparent that any attempt to exclude values from the curriculum can result only in monumental deficiencies in our children's preparation for life. Just as it is crucial to understand the laws of gravity, magnetism, and acceleration before someone is prepared to become an engineer, so it is essential to develop qualities like cooperation, cheerfulness, and concentration before someone can hope to find success and fulfillment in life.

Values are also universal in the common experiences that accompany their practice. Among the most familiar examples are the joy that can be found in helping others, the satisfaction that comes from doing our best, and the tranquility felt when telling the truth. In his wry manner, Mark Twain once referred to this latter correlation with the comment, "If you don't lie, you don't have to remember anything." These experiences are found in every culture and religion and provide a source of intrinsic motivation for continually practicing the qualities. Of course, it is also apparent that not everyone experiences these feelings with the same degree of intensity. Levels of awareness that provide a lifetime of motivation for a Mother Teresa, a Martin Luther King, or a Mahatma Gandhi may be only dimly perceived by some people and wholly unknown to others.

The Progressive Development Model

These variations in the ability to sense subtler feelings hold tremendous significance for teachers and parents. Why do some people experience deep fulfillment in the act of sharing while others steal without the slightest remorse? In our school we account for these discrepancies through the model of Progressive Development. From this perspective, children move along a spectrum of awareness that encompasses three basic stages: heavy, ego-active, and light.

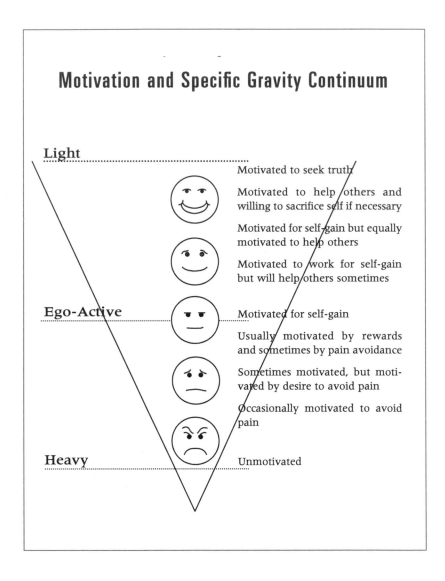

Motivation and Specific Gravity Continuum

Light
- Motivated to seek truth
- Motivated to help others and willing to sacrifice self if necessary
- Motivated for self-gain but equally motivated to help others
- Motivated to work for self-gain but will help others sometimes

Ego-Active
- Motivated for self-gain
- Usually motivated by rewards and sometimes by pain avoidance
- Sometimes motivated, but motivated by desire to avoid pain
- Occasionally motivated to avoid pain

Heavy
- Unmotivated

The heavy or lower end of the spectrum is marked by a sluggish, contractive disposition that masks any perception of the finer values. In the ego-active range there is an energetic involvement in life that is confined to self-serving, materialistic concerns. The light or upper level is characterized by a dynamic, expansive spirit that reaches out in an ever-widening concern for the well-being of others. The Spectrum of Awareness in Appendix A of this book provides examples of how various kinds of behavior fit along this continuum.

Progressive Development helps teachers adjust their actions to meet a variety of student needs. At the heavy end of the spectrum students lack the capacity for appreciating the subtler benefits of good behavior. Their heavy consciousness requires a more explicit motivational system that controls their behavior through clearly defined checks and restraints. Here the immediate goal is to find ways of increasing the general level of energy, a step that eventually leads to higher levels of awareness. In the ego-active stage, the goal is to directly awaken higher sensitivities through an approach that follows Shakespeare's dictum: "Assume a virtue though you have it not." Here, the teacher creates an environment that rewards positive choices. At first students demonstrate good behavior solely to obtain the outward rewards, but gradually they begin to appreciate the increased level of well-being the behavior itself brings. Children at the light level of consciousness can sense the intrinsic rewards of positive values. Teachers, therefore, need offer only gentle reminders and an ongoing source of support.

The Tools of Maturity

A related component of our school's philosophy concerns the development of what we refer to as the child's four Tools of Maturity: the body, feelings, will, and intellect.

The Tools of Maturity

There are four aspects of one's being that need to be specifically developed in a balanced and harmonious way: body, feeling, will power, and intellect.

Physical Energy and Control

To develop can care for the body for its long-term usage.

Emotional Calmness and Expansivemess

To learn to harness and channel turbulent emotions and develop calm sensitive feelings as an invaluable tool of understanding.

Dynamic and Persistent Will Power

To learn to focus one's energies towards overcoming obstacles and achieving success.

Clear, Practical Intellect

To develop clarity of thought.

's' Sake

By cultivating these tools in a balanced and harmonious way, a teacher can greatly enhance a child's ability to discover and appreciate higher values. When the body is healthy and well exercised, the child has the energy necessary for growth of all kinds. Calm, sensitive feelings provide for a deeper awareness of one's own motives and reactions as well as a clearer insight into the needs of others. Through the development of the will, the child learns to focus one-pointed, persistent energy toward the realization of a goal. Finally, a clear, strong intellect is necessary for analyzing a situation and determining a reasonable response. A deficiency in any of these four areas produces a serious handicap in a child's ability to cultivate positive values.

The development of these tools is associated with natural stages of childhood, somewhat akin to those described by Maria Montessori and Rudolf Steiner. For physical development (the body and senses) this period is from 0 to 6 years of age, for the intellect, from 18 to 24 years. The focus of this book is on the remaining two stages, feeling and will, which cover the elementary and high school years.

Between the ages of 6 and 12, children have a capacity for looking at their feelings with a degree of objectivity not possible in earlier years. This age is also relatively free of the strong identification with a particular style of behavior that occurs a little later in life. Thus, there is a special opportunity for constructive work, especially with the more turbulent emotions of anger, greed, hatred, and jealousy. At the same time, these children can also deepen their awareness of the calm, inner feeling that is known as intuition. Many exercises described in chapter 2 have the goal of developing greater sensitivity and control of feelings. Activities for cultivating intuition and inner peace are described in the chapter five.

The years from 12 to 18 spotlight the development of the will. It is easy to observe the teenager's need to step out into broader, more challenging aspects of life. It is the responsibility of adults to provide opportunities for meeting this need in healthy, life-affirming ways. The service adventures presented in the previous chapter have certainly provided this kind of challenge for our students. The need for money offers another simple and almost universal opportunity for developing the will. A teenager's broadened awareness of the world is often accompanied by an increased desire for clothes, electronic equipment, and travel. Earning at least part of the money for such items is an ideal way of developing will power.

For those interested in a more thorough presentation of the Progressive Development model and the Tools of Maturity, along with many other valuable points, I strongly recommend the book *Education for Life* by J. Donald Walters*. The book is filled with helpful insights into the moral and spiritual growth of children and serves as the
ok for the development of our school.

nmary then, a sectarian approach to values creates
ary obstacles in working with children. If values
ble only to a select few, then the goal must be to

Sake

indoctrinate everyone into the particular beliefs of that group. From this perspective values must be approached as a kind of implant on an otherwise morally deficient population. From the universal view, however, values are seen as an integral part of life's basic infrastructure. As such, our primary concern is to support children in their process of exploration, especially through the kinds of training described in the next chapter. As children broaden and refine their experiences, they will gradually deepen their appreciation of the importance of values.

* Walters, J. Donald, 1997, *Education for Life*, Nevada City, CA: Crystal Clarity Publishers

Excerpts from the World's Great Scriptures

From the New Testament

Galatians 5:22–23

> *But the fruit of the Spirit is love, joy, peace, long suffering, gentleness, goodness, faith, meekness, temperance: against such there is no law.*

Luke 6:36–38

> *Be ye therefore merciful, as your Father also is merciful. Judge not, and ye shall not be judged: condemn not, and ye shall not be condemned: forgive, and ye shall be forgiven: Give, and it shall be given unto you; good measure, pressed down, and shaken together, and running over, shall men give into your bosom. For with the same measure that ye mete withal it shall be measured to you again.*

From 100 Sayings of Confucius: 39

Confucius said,

> *"The gentleman [man of moral integrity] has nine considerations: he aims at clearness in seeing, acuteness in hearing, mildness in countenance, politeness in manners, sincerity in speech, earnestness in action, consulting others when in doubt, thinking of the consequences when angry, and thinking of rightness at the sight of gain."*

the Qur'an

who spend (benevolently) in ease as well as in strait-
nd those who restrain (their) anger and pardon men;

ake

and Allah loves the doers of good (to others).

4.114:

There is no good in most of their secret counsels except (in his) who enjoins charity or goodness or reconciliation between people; and whoever does this seeking Allah's pleasure, we will give him a mighty reward.

90.17:

Then he is of those who believe and charge one another to show patience, and charge one another to show compassion.

From the Old Testament

Zechariah 7:9

Thus speaketh the LORD of hosts, saying, Execute true judgment, and shew mercy and compassions every man to his brother:

Proverbs 12:19

The lip of truth shall be established forever: but a lying tongue is but for a moment.

From the Bhagavad Gita

16:1–3

Fearlessness, purity of heart, perseverance in (acquiring) wisdom and in (practicing) yoga, charity, subjugation of the senses, performance of holy rites, study of the scriptures, self-discipline, straightforwardness;

Non-injury, truthfulness, freedom from wrath, renunciation, peacefulness, non-slanderousness, compassion for all creatures, absence of greed, gentleness, modesty, lack of restlessness;

Radiance of character, forgiveness, patience, cleanness, freedom from hate, absence of conceit—these qualities are the wealth of a divinely inclined person.

5

From
Restlessness
to Self-Discovery

In my work with children I have
found that restlessness is the greatest obstacle to the discov-
ery of values. Qualities like honesty, kindness, and even
courage, though powerful and enduring in their effects,
can be easily overlooked amidst the tension and noise of
daily life. For some, restlessness stems from emotional or
physical trauma, for others, an unhealthy diet, especially
one with an excess of sugar. The most common problem,
however, is over-stimulation: the result of too much expo-
sure to videos, computer games, music, and TV.

To help children develop the deeper sensitivity necessary
for the appreciation of values, it is important to work

※

directly on the root issue of restlessness. In introducing this approach, I often use the following metaphor:

> *Imagine a beautiful lake with a strong wind blowing across its surface. When you first look at the water, all you can see are the rippling waves that the wind has created. Now watch closely as the wind subsides. Gradually the waves diminish, revealing an ever-clearer reflection of a full moon shining above the lake. The moon was there from the beginning, but was initially hidden by the turbulence on the lake's surface.*

The values we would share are already present, much like the moon above the lake. If we can help children calm the turbulence of their bodies and minds, they will be able to recognize these values in the same way they recognize old friends.

Yoga, introspection, and meditation are the most effective tools I have found for helping children develop sensitivity and subtler awareness. Although yoga and meditation may provoke controversy with some people, the descriptions that follow should demonstrate how naturally they fit into a nonsectarian, nondogmatic program. One simple activity that facilitates inner calmness involves listening to soothing, beautiful music while coloring mandalas (symmetrical geometric shapes). Another example uses a small set of chimes. After striking a chime, ask the children to close their eyes and listen carefully until the last vestige of sound disappears.

While working with a particularly restless group of teenagers, I challenged them to focus their minds one pointedly for five minutes. To give them a way of measuring progress, I rang a small bell at 30-second intervals. The students counted one point each time the bell rang if they were still concentrating. At the end of each session, students filled out individual charts, keeping track of their total number of points. At the end of the second week, the class asked if I would stop ringing the bell because it interrupted their concentration! The experience of inner focus had become self-rewarding.

Another occasion reminded me why working with young people can be so challenging and so satisfying at the same time. I was leading a group of teenagers through a series of yoga classes that were benefiting most of the students. One girl, however (the most restless person in the class), seemed untouched by what we were doing. In searching for a way to help her, I came up with a little experiment. At the end of the next session, I asked everyone to remain lying on the floor while I came around to test each one by gently moving an arm or leg. I explained that the relative flexibility or limpness of a limb would be a good indicator of the student's level of relaxation. As I made my way around the room, the students all showed satisfactory results until I came to the girl. When I lifted her right leg slightly and then released it, it remained suspended in the air! Somehow she'd never connected the concept of relaxation to a particular physical sensation. With a little extra help, she finally got the idea. Since then I've often added the "limp limb" test to our relaxation sessions.

The following activities help children overcome physical and mental restlessness through balance, physical relaxation, mental relaxation, and meditation. As with the qualities in chapter two, I have listed suggested age ranges, group sizes, and levels of use.

The Goal of Balance
Ages: 5–17; Group Size: 1–35; Level of Use: Introductory

Physical balance is a skill related to concentration. The essence of both activities is the ability to stay focused amidst a variety of distractions. In general, it is easier for a child to develop a skill first on the physical plane before applying it to more abstract mental and social levels.

ACTIVITY: *Immovable Warrior*
Divide the children into pairs. Each child then stands with feet together and palms upraised, facing his or her opponent at a distance of one to two feet. The objective is to cause the other child to lose balance by slapping palms against the opponent's palms. Feinting is a good strategy, but touching any other part of the opponent's body is grounds for disqualification. The first child to move either foot even slightly loses. Surprisingly, size is not an advantage in this exercise. Often small children have been able to dislodge bigger ones.

ACTIVITY: *Immovable Warrior, Advanced Mode*

The children face each other as in Immovable Warrior, but this time standing on one foot and raising only one palm toward their opponent. (Show them how by raising one foot behind you and grasping it with the hand of the same side.) Opponents need to mirror each another so opposite palms are raised. Any movement of the balance foot or touching anything except the opponent's palm ends the round.

Student and teacher demonstrating
the warrior pose

ACTIVITY: *The Tree Pose*

In this traditional yogic pose, the children stand and place all their weight on their right foot. Tell them to visualize themselves as trees with deep roots stretching into the ground beneath their foot. Next, have them pick out a stationary object (not another person) across the room and keep their eyes fixed on that spot. Now have them carefully lift the left foot and rest it on the inside of the right knee. Finally, ask them to slowly lift the palms until they can be held together above the head. After resting in a normal standing position, have the children assume the tree pose balancing on the left foot. I'd suggest you start with a goal of 30 seconds and gradually extend the period as your students develop skill. Look for an opportunity to point out how mental relaxation helps with the ability to stay balanced.

With some groups, competition provides a helpful stimulus. To have a contest, ring a bell so that everyone starts together. Keep track of how long each person holds the pose. Add up all the times for a composite score. The children can then try to break their record at the next session.

The Goal of Physical Relaxation
Ages: 5–17; Group Size: 1–35; Level of Use: Introductory

Perhaps surprisingly, deep relaxation is the most popular activity in this entire book. I have seen it work wonders even with very restless groups of children. It may have to do with the frenetic pace of most children's lives, or perhaps that of our society in general, but everyone enjoys the experience of peace. Through sharing periods of calmness and harmony with their friends, a tone is set that has a positive effect on the children's other interactions.

Student practicing Tree Pose during Yosemite trip

ACTIVITY: *Deep Relaxation*

Have your group lie on the carpet or, better yet, on mats or blankets. Play some quiet, soothing, instrumental music. Have the children inhale and tense every muscle in their bodies, then exhale and relax. Repeat this procedure two or three times. After the final exhalation, tell them to let their breath flow naturally while they close their eyes and follow the visualization you are going to lead.

Imagine that you are floating on an ocean of peace. With every breath, feel that a wave of peace is gently flowing through your body, dissolving all tensions, fears, and worries. Begin by seeing waves of peace washing over your toes and feet. Now these waves are flowing up through your ankles and calves, releasing all tension. Next, feel the waves of peace all around your knees and thighs, and then up through your hips and around your abdomen and stomach. Feel the entire lower half of your body completely relaxed.

Now concentrate on your fingers and hands, feeling the waves of peace there. Let the feeling of calmness flow up through your wrists and forearms. Next feel this cool, refreshing energy all around your elbows and up into your biceps. The next wave washes through your shoulders and then all around your back and chest, releasing every worry, every concern.

Finally feel waves of peace flowing up through your neck and throat. Follow the flow of peace around your entire face, bringing relaxation to your chin, lips, tongue, and cheeks. Watch it move on through your nose, ears, and eyes, and then up through your forehead, top of the head, and brain. Your entire body is now one continuous wave of peace, floating on an ocean of peace. You are perfectly safe, free of all cares and worries. Rest in this state and realize that it is an essential part of who you are.

The foregoing is, of course, only a suggestion. Adapt the words in any way that fits your group's needs. Lead the visualization at a speed you feel comfortable with, mentioning the body parts you want the children to relax and reminding them of the growing feelings of peace, harmony, and calmness. The entire exercise can take from 5 to 10 minutes. At the end of the visualization, let the children lie quietly for a minute or two. To end the session, have everyone inhale deeply, tense every muscle gently, relax, and slowly come up to a sitting position.

Students practicing relaxation yoga pose

There are hundreds of yoga postures that have the goal of cultivating physical relaxation. It can be very beneficial to lead your group through a few of them before using the Deep Relaxation exercise.

ACTIVITY: *Quick Relaxation*

When you want an extra degree of attention, or if the group has simply become too restless, have everyone stand up. Ask the children to inhale with a deep breath, holding it for five seconds while they tense every muscle in their bodies. Tell them to exhale completely and relax. Repeat three to five times. You may want to teach your children how to take in a really deep breath by expanding not only the chest but also the stomach and rib cage. (See the Goal of Meditation later in this chapter.)

The Goal of Mental Relaxation

Ages: 5–17; Group Size: 1–35; Level of Use: Established; Preparation Needed

Many children can study with a parent or teacher by their side, but are easily distracted when left on their own. The following exercise produces a state of conscious, mental relaxation. From this point of rest, children can learn to take control of their minds, realizing that they can choose which sensory stimuli to attend to. In addition to improving concentration, this skill contributes to greater health and well being through the ability to release stress.

ACTIVITY: *Sand Trays*

(materials needed for each child: one tray with enough clean sand to fill each tray to a depth of at least one inch, two or three small stones or marbles, and a short stick for raking. Trays should be about 8 inches square, preferably with a lid that will help keep the sand clean.)

Prepare the trays and hand them out to the children. Tell them there will be a series of stages to the exercise and that you will ring a bell (or make some other sound) as you announce the next stage.

Stage One: Everyone talks while they begin drawing in their sand trays.

Stage Two: Children continue drawing, but in silence (verbal silence).

Stage Three: Children continue drawing, but move toward deeper silence by keeping their eyes focused on the sand, letting go of all other thoughts (mental silence).

Stage Four: Children continue to draw in the state of mental silence, but with eyes closed, trying to become aware of an inner sense of peace.

Stage Five: With the eyes closed and the mind focused on inner peace, children stop drawing or moving.

Time the exercise to meet the attention span of your children, but one to two minutes is a good duration for each step. Depending on your group, you may want to work on only the first couple of stages for awhile. When the children show definite signs of calmness, move into stages three, four, and five. Soothing background music can enhance the effects of this activity.

When children have developed some skill at this exercise, you can introduce variations such as colored sand and other small objects. Japanese rock gardens and Tibetan sand mandalas are two examples of highly refined extensions of this activity. You could also ask everyone to express what they are feeling through a picture, poem, dance, or story.

The Goal of Meditation
Ages: 5–17; Group Size: 1–35; Level of Use: Established

Meditation is a skill that builds on all the preceding practices and can produce profound states of inner peace and joy. Although often associated with Buddhist or Hindu traditions, there are many references to meditative practice in the Christian, Jewish, Muslim, and other religions. I share it with my children as simply a practice that leads to heightened inner awareness.

ACTIVITY: *Meditation*
Preparation:

- Teach the children diaphragmatic breathing by asking them to sit quietly with one hand on the stomach and the other on the chest. On the next inhalation ask them to note which hand moves first. Usually it will be the one on the chest. Point out that beginning the breath with the stomach (diaphragm) and extending the inhalation up through the ribs and then into the chest produces a fuller breath and a greater sense of relaxation that is helpful in meditation.
- Discuss the importance of good posture. A straight spine with shoulders slightly back and the chin level to the ground helps keep the attention alert. This posture can be attained in several ways, including sitting cross-legged on the floor with or without a pillow, using a kneeling bench, or sitting on the front edge of a chair. Let the children choose the position that is most comfortable for them.

✳

- Because meditation is done with closed eyes, there can be a tendency toward drowsiness. To help keep the mind uplifted and alert, teach the children to focus their attention gently upward toward the point between the eyebrows.
- Finally, ask them to choose a short saying, or mantra, from a list that includes I am light, I am peace, I am love, I am joy, and I am energy.

Students practicing meditation

Practice:

The session begins with measured breathing. I lead two or three cycles of inhalation, holding the breath, and exhalation, with each stage lasting for a count of six. Then we move on to breath counting. Here the children relax and allow their breathing to proceed at a natural pace. I tell them to observe their bodies, just as if they were watching someone else breathe, while they count 5 to 10 breaths.

Student meditating at the Grand Canyon

For the third exercise I ask them to mentally recite their mantra 10–15 times, using a pace of one recitation per breath. To end the session I ask the children to sit quietly, inwardly feeling the quality expressed in their mantra.

The length of our meditation depends on the group, but five minutes is a good beginning for children ages nine and up. With teenagers, we've built up to 20 minutes or more. In general, I try to guide the first part of the meditation, leaving the last third for quiet enjoyment of the interiorized state of awareness. I often use the Meditation chart, which I hand out at the end of each session. In it the children keep track of the number of breaths and mantra recitations as well as their level of concentration.

✳

See Appendix B: Charts, page 144, for the Meditation Chart. To use this chart, copy it on a photocopy machine at 129% increase.

For more ideas on meditating, especially with younger children, I recommend *Supporting Your Child's Inner Life* by Toby Moorhouse. (Ananda Living Wisdom School, 530-478-7640)

Students' Comments

I asked some of my junior and senior high school students to comment on our practice of yoga and meditation. Their observations follow.

> *"I think that yoga has affected me in a lot of good ways. I almost always feel calm and nice after yoga or meditation.*
>
> *"The daily periods of yoga and meditation help me to focus through the whole day. Meditation provides me with clarity and peace for learning."*
>
> *"In the morning we have yoga and meditation. I'm feeling really good because I'm more awake after this. It's really silent here; I think it's better for learning."*
>
> *"Meditation helps me calm down and start the morning that way. I love doing deep relaxation because it helps me focus my mind."*

"When we meditate in class it's a good way to start the day. It helps my stress and tiredness from the morning and gets me into a calm mode."

"Yoga exercises helps me think better during the day and they also make me feel better and not so tired."

"I like yoga because it helps my energy. I try to meditate but I sometimes have trouble calming my mind and slowing down my thoughts. If I can't concentrate, I talk to God about what's going on in my life and ask him to help me with certain things like temper, not to argue, and other things."

"Meditation calms me down and makes me feel good."

"Meditation feels good because you get to be more in tune with God."

"I think that when we meditate as a class it calms us down a lot. I wouldn't be surprised if it helps our whole day be more harmonious."

6

The Role
of Adults

Relationships

This book's subtitle, *Helping Children and Teens Discover Life's Higher Values,* implies a relationship between adults and children based upon mutual respect. Whenever I present a workshop on these principles and techniques, I try to provide an opportunity for each adult to spend one-on-one time with a child. While it seems obvious that this would be a prerequisite for anyone wanting to work with children, my experience with teacher training programs is that the emphasis is almost always on group dynamics and curriculum, seldom on relating to an individual child. In our sessions the adult-child pair is given 45 minutes to an hour of free time, ideally in a natural setting. The goal for the adult is simply to become reacquainted with some of the treasures of childhood. Although the lack of structure is threatening for some adults, this session is often the highlight of the workshop. Common observations include a renewed appreciation for the timelessness of childhood, its spontaneity, creativity, purity, and trust. When adults can truly appreciate the gifts of childhood, there is a basis for a dynamic and fruitful relationship that is richly rewarding for everyone. In this context, it is natural for children to open themselves willingly to the guidance adults can offer.

Here are a few guidelines I've found helpful, both as parent and teacher, for building positive relationships with children.

1. Be on the lookout for spontaneous opportunities for one-on-one contact (walking together, the need for special help, etc.) while also planning structured times as needed (teachers can use a quiet reading period, parents can schedule special daddy-daughter, etc., times).

2. Keep the lines of communication open through sincere interest and honest sharing (as opposed to superficial comments or indifference) about their everyday accomplishments.

3. Balance advice-giving with at least equal amounts of listening. It's amazing how often I've had a child tell me in his or her own words exactly what I was planning to say.

4. Look for ideas that you can support. Even the attempt to make use of their ideas gives a strong message of respect.

5. Find ways of spending time together that you can both enjoy. Relationships built on activities that only you or your child enjoys will be unfulfilling.

6. Create situations where children are comfortable sharing their feelings, but never pry. Trust must be given freely; it can never be produced on demand. Some of the most important sharing will happen spontaneously during quiet one-on-one activities.

7. Find creative little ways to show your interest and concern (a beautiful leaf, a personal note, an unexpected hug, etc.).

8. Stop briefly when a child asks for your attention during a busy time, establish eye contact as you pause to explain why you can't stop longer, and then make a point of getting back to the child.

9. Identify specific qualities in each child that you can honestly admire. Keep your thoughts and words focused on these positive attributes while avoiding unnecessary negative comments, especially in front of their peers and even when talking to other adults.

10. Occasionally relate to them in a spontaneous, playful way. We all carry traces of our childhood within us. It's beneficial for both you and the child to let these traces slip out sometimes.

11. Allow each relationship to unfold naturally, steadily offering your respect and interest while waiting patiently for a genuine response.
12. Pray for your children's growth; visualize them shining with light and love.

Firm, Loving Discipline

Even the best adult-child relationship requires occasional discipline, but here, too, there are principles that promote open, respectful interactions. Foremost among these basics is appreciating the difference between true discipline and raw displays of power. Everyone has witnessed scenes in the grocery store or other public place in which a child is being punished, not for doing anything wrong, but only because the behavior hasn't matched the parent's desire. This kind of interaction is guaranteed to create either rebellion or obsequious submission and is to be avoided whenever possible. Discipline is defined as "training that is expected to produce a specified character or pattern of behavior, especially that which is expected to produce moral or mental improvement." It is in this sense of moral improvement that discipline plays an important, even crucial role in sharing values.

My first years of teaching were characterized by two related flaws: I lacked confidence in my disciplinary skills and was overly concerned with being liked by my students. As a result behavior problems grew to the point where I remember purchasing a set of boxing gloves as a desperate means of getting the children to work out their difficulties. Fortunately, it was then that I realized that the problems weren't so much in the children as they were in me. A little introspection revealed that I really did know when I should intervene (the growing knots in my stomach were pretty clear evidence); I was just hesitant to do so. Once I started to take action, the discipline problems quickly began to subside (sparing me the cost of expensive ulcer medications as well as the trouble of undertaking a career as a boxing coach). Most surprising for me was the shift in the children's attitude. Although I had been concerned that discipline would cause the children to dislike me, I immediately observed an increase in their level of respect and appreciation. It was in this way that I realized the importance of firm, loving discipline in a child's life.

Children, like the rest of us, become confused at times about the proper course of action. Nature has arranged it, however, so that children are normally surrounded by adults who have greater life experience and, hopefully, greater wisdom. Adults who have developed their own calm, inner feeling are able to sense when a child has lost focus and can intervene to help the child regain self-control. This kind of intervention not only improves the child's behavior, but also lends reassurance that there is someone who will step in and help if things start to get out of hand. The sense of security that results from this kind of discipline manifests as emotional and even physical relaxation in the child. Conversely, children who are not well disciplined become restless and tense, often displaying a lack of respect for adults whom they rightly sense are not fulfilling a primary responsibility.

It was at this point that I began to discover my five keys to good discipline: individualize, pay attention, simplify, minimize, and follow through.

1. Individualize

As we saw in Chapter Four, children operate along a spectrum of Progressive Development from heavy, to ego-active, to light. Good discipline will recognize which level a child is functioning on and respond accordingly. A student helped me immensely in grasping this point. Daniel was often conflicted by moods. Although I was concerned, I found myself in a quandary because sometimes I was able to help and at other times I wasn't. During one of his better periods, we sat down to talk about the situation. I explained my dilemma, and Daniel explained his situation in an amazingly mature and succinct manner. He said, "If I catch the beginning of a mood, it's like I'm dusty and only have to brush myself off. If I wait longer, it's like I'm muddy and have to work much harder to get clean. If I forget to pay attention, it's like I'm stuck in the tar pits and have to just sit there until the mood passes."

Thus it is with awareness in general. With heavy awareness it is first necessary to increase the level of energy, usually through strong negative motivation (extra work, loss of freedom, or other unpleasant consequence). At the ego-active stage, more energy is needed to motivate change and improvement, usually in the form of a reward external to the situation (extra privileges, toys, food, etc.).

At the highest, light end of the spectrum there are only minor mists that temporarily obscure clear vision. A gentle reminder is often all that is needed. Discipline that is out-of-phase with the child's level of awareness is ineffective and often counterproductive. For example, heavy consequences for a child operating at a light level will produce confusion and hurt feelings. Conversely, light reminders for children at heavier levels will simply be ignored.

2. Pay Attention

This point sounds so simple, but it makes a world of difference. Children's misbehaviors are somewhat akin to weather systems. They begin as smallish squalls, but can grow into full-fledged storms. When I started teaching I was often preoccupied with lesson plans, classroom visitors, and other distractions. As a result my discipline problems tended to be of the hurricane variety, with people yelling at each other or throwing things. When I finally decided to pay primary attention to my students, I began to notice the slight deviations of behavior that, like Daniel's "dusty" stage, required only a little energy to straighten out.

3. Simplify

Good discipline is hard enough to implement without introducing unnecessary complications. For example, disciplining a child in front of peers complicates things. Now the child is thinking not only about the discipline, but also how his or her friends are going to react. Here we see the "playing to the masses" syndrome when the punishment is far less important than looking good, and can even reinforce the negative behavior because of increased peer approval. Generally, discipline should be meted out in private, as quickly after the incident as possible.

4. Minimize

Just because some discipline is good doesn't necessarily mean that more is better. In fact, I have found that the reverse tends to be true. In any given situation I, as an adult, have a certain "quota" of interventions that can be helpful. If I go beyond this number, even though my intentions are still good, the overriding impact is negative (nagging, intrusion, etc.). Therefore, it is important to reserve discipline for the most important issues. If a child's behavior is generally moving in the right direction, let borderline incidents slide, either by ignoring them or showing only mild interest. If things escalate, then intervene. With young children a simple change of environment may be all that is required. Finally, if children aren't in danger of serious harm, allow mistakes to happen. They can offer invaluable opportunities for growth.

5. Follow Through

One of the greatest abuses of discipline is to lay down a boundary or consequence and then not enforce it. For example, you might say, "Johnny, if you throw anything you'll have to go to your room." Johnny then throws a pencil and you say, "Johnny, I thought I told you not to throw things." And then, no follow through. You've just taught Johnny and any other child within a 10-mile radius that they don't have to listen to you. You will then find your voice growing hoarse from repeating yourself at gradually louder volumes as you establish yourself as a totally ineffective parent or teacher. The cure? Think before you verbalize a consequence. Do you really intend to enforce it in just the way you state it? If the answer is no, keep quiet. When you really mean what you say, then, and only then, speak.

Sensitive, appropriate discipline is tremendously important in helping children discover higher values. Children usually know when they are misbehaving. Appropriate intervention therefore reinforces their innate sense of justice and awakens their respect for wisdom. In a similar way, children can also sense injustice. So, what do you do when you realize that you misread a situation, punished the wrong kid, or were too heavy in your response? Apologize! Sometimes this response, more than any thing else, will convince children that you are trying to act only from your highest perceptions.

Setting Priorities

Along with relationships and discipline, the desire to emphasize values is all that is needed to get things going. It is a fact that whatever we consider important is what we notice. I remember being amazed, after taking a temporary job as a postman, at the tremendous variety of mailboxes. About the same time I bought a small white car and immediately began noticing how many other small white cars there were. In working with children, our priorities exercise a similar effect on our minds. Test scores, dance performances, college acceptance, sports events—there are many focal points that can dominate our interactions with children. When we make values the priority, we become aware of many previously unnoticed possibilities. For example, with the snow recess described in the opening chapter, my focus on cooperation helped me see an important opportunity for learning in what would otherwise have passed by as just another unhappy recess.

Whenever values are emphasized, opportunities for sharing them abound. Math becomes a laboratory for building will power and perseverance, tests and homework a proving ground for honesty, the playground a workshop in kindness and cooperation . . . . Setting a particular tone will draw the students into a similar mindset. On a recent trip to Zion National Park, the spirit of challenge was in the air as we drove to the trailhead for a session of solitary hiking. As we approached a long tunnel, the boys spontaneously challenged themselves to see if they could hold their breath until we got to the other end. One minute and forty-five seconds later we emerged from the tunnel to the cheers of several air-deprived, but delighted students.

A determined focus on values can sometimes seem inconvenient. Although we can schedule times for stories, activities, and even adventures, the really special moments tend to appear out of the blue and demand immediate attention. At these times I try to remind myself that "Life cannot be viewed as a disruption to a lesson plan." Rather,

I must be willing to harmonize my agenda to the flow of life. I have to admit, though, that often my first reaction to these special events is to recoil at the unexpected difficulties or inharmonious situations. I then turn to another of my favorite sayings: "There are no such things as obstacles, only opportunities". This shift of perspective allows me to look at the incident in a new light. Usually I find that we have been presented with just the conditions we need.

Getting Started

If you've gotten this far in the book, hopefully you agree that values are worth sharing and that it's at least theoretically possible to do it. The final question, then, is how to get started. Taking up a challenge of this kind can seem somewhat daunting. I'm reminded of a friend who was completing his medical internship with a tour of duty as the only doctor in an emergency room. On his first shift he was more than a little apprehensive, especially when the first ambulance pulled up and a badly injured man was deposited on his examination table. He said the first thought that popped into his mind was, "Oh my God, this person needs a doctor!"

I had a similar reaction when confronted with my first challenge in working with values. It was only a day or two into the school year when it became clear to me that Peter, one of my six-year olds, was incapable of telling the difference between lying and telling the truth. My first reaction was to call in a psychologist. Then, remembering our

※

school's meager budget, I realized there wouldn't be anyone else to help.

Left to my own devices, the only thing that popped into my mind was the story of Pinocchio. I would have dismissed this idea as silly except that I couldn't come up with anything better. So, with minimal expectations I checked the book out of the library. The next day I began reading it to the class during story time, seating myself so I could observe Peter's reaction. The story immediately captured his attention, and with each succeeding page Peter's eyes seemed to get bigger. Later, I called him aside to talk about the story, and we got onto the topic of lying and the truth. He agreed that he had difficulty knowing the difference, and we worked out a simple plan of action. Each day at lunch recess I would observe his behavior for 5 or 10 minutes. Then I would call him over and ask him what he had been doing. At first he would tell me about the elephants and pirates and other outlandish things he had seen. I would respond, "No, I was watching and that didn't happen." When he mentioned something that really had taken place, I'd corroborate his observation. Amazingly, this approach worked beautifully. In a little more than two weeks, Peter's problem had disappeared.

I relate this story and the next one as reassurance that it isn't necessary to have all the answers before you start. Help can come in quite unexpected ways. Some years later I was working with a group of very active adolescents. Because of an usually rainy winter and the fact that our school had no gymnasium, my students were beginning to feel trapped in our small classroom. One day a woman asked if she could observe in our class. I welcomed her and showed her to a seat at the back of the room. Later that morning the students and I got into a serious discussion of what to do with all the bottled up energy. Someone mentioned snow camping as a possibility because we live only an hour or so below the snowline. I said I thought it was an excellent idea, except that I didn't know the first thing about snow camping or how to go about researching it. (This was in the days before search engines and the internet.) At this point our visitor raised her hand and asked if she could speak. She told us that she was the nearest thing to a professional snowcamper we were likely to find and had led many expeditions of this sort. She said her schedule wouldn't allow her to accompany us, but that she could tell us everything we needed to know for a successful experience. Three days later the class and I were up in the High Sierras digging a 5-foot high, 15-foot circumference snow cave that proved to be warmer than expected and quite satisfying to my group of young adventurers!

The lesson for me in both situations is that when the need becomes clear, the solution is just around the corner. Before our first Mexico trip, the students' need for a broader life experience was obvious. Questions were immediately raised about safety, finances, what we would do during our visit, and whether this activity qualified as a proper use of school time. Each of these issues raised the possibility of stopping our plans before we started. However, by moving ahead into admittedly unknown territory, every obstacle melted away.

Except for a few cases of Montezuma's Revenge (intestinal problems), we had no serious injuries or illness. Living in an orphanage answered our need for inexpensive room and board and provided more than enough activity for the students. As far as scholastic achievement, the first hand experience of another culture was clearly worth months of bookwork.

The challenge, then, is clear. Children thrive on an experiential approach to values. All they need is the help of a caring, sensitive adult. This book describes the basic guidelines for implementing an effective program. Now you just need to find one likely candidate from your area to get things started . . . .

Conclusion

Cheerfulness, Forgiveness, Courage, Even-mindedness, Concentration, Patience, Integrity, Sensitivity, Trust, Cooperation, Sincerity, Will Power, Peace, Compassion, Self-Control, Enthusiasm, Honesty,

Love, Joy—the words fairly shine on the printed page. These are the jewels of human existence. What greater gift can we offer our children than the opportunity to discover and cultivate these qualities?

As our world grows closer together, we can more easily realize that these qualities are a part of everyone's heritage, no matter what our religious or cultural background. As such they offer us a basis for emphasizing the oneness of the human race. On an individual level, these qualities contribute mightily to each person's sense of self-worth and fulfillment.

As parents and teachers, we have the opportunity to facilitate our children's growth through sharing activities like the ones described in this book. Children who go through such a program will learn to integrate values into their lives, not out of fear of an authority figure or the desire to impress others, but because they have seen through direct, personal experience that values improve the quality of their lives. In this way they become prepared for the ongoing process of refining their understanding and deepening their appreciation of values through the countless lessons that life will place before them.

In closing, I'd like to share what I consider one of the highest compliments someone could offer a program of this kind. It came from an administrator from another school who had worked with several of our students. She told one of the mothers, "I'd like to come and visit your school. I'm impressed with your students. They're different. They know who they are."

Appendix A: The Spectrum of Awareness

Spectrum of Awareness

Adapted from the Psychological Chart by Paramhansa Yogananda (refer to chapter four for context)

HEAVY (Contractive)

Moral and Spiritual Attitudes

1) Lacks a sense for doing what's right

2) Impervious to reason, obstinate

3) Superstitious

4) Fears authority

Social Relationships

1) Shows hypocritical sympathy

2) Shy

3) Callous, heartless

4) Deceiving

5) Lustful

6) Treacherous

7) Easily led or influenced by others

Personal Style of Behavior

1) Habitually untruthful

2) Quiet, dull

3) Attachment to possessions

4) Procrastinates

5) Morose, moody

6) Careless, negligent

7) Crooked—finds undesirable meanings in things

8) Covetous

9) Has a propensity to steal

✳

10) Has a begging nature

11) Lacks self-confidence

12) Dutiful out of fear of punishment

13) Lacks self-respect

EGO-ACTIVE (Agitated)

Moral and Spiritual Attitudes

1) Susceptible to correction if there is personal gain

2) Prompt in forming resolutions but not persistent in carrying them out

3) Tries to please those in authority for personal advantage

4) Capable of repentance if reminded of one's own or others' past misfortune

Social Relationships

1) Shows partiality

2) Selfish

3) Fickle

4) Imitative

5) Meddling

6) Revengeful

7) Faultfinding

8) Quarrelsome

9) Garrulous

Personal Style of Behavior

1) Untruthful out of impulse, out of fun, out of exaggerating tendency

2) Truthfulness with selfish motive

3) Shrewd

4) Fastidious

5) Easily despondent, melancholy

6) Ambitious

7) Maudlin

8) Turbulent, impulsive

9) Proud

10) Dutiful out of hope of reward

11) Overly serious

LIGHT (Expansive)

Moral and Spiritual Attitudes

1) Self-disciplined

2) Reforming spirit

3) Sense for doing what's right

4) Acts in accordance with the suggestions of superior minds

5) Reverence for Divine subjects

6) Love for good qualities

7) Admiration for great men and women

Social Relationships

1) Love toward animals

2) Love for parents and friends

3) Practical sympathy for others

4) Benevolent tendency toward the needy

5) Tender

6) Faithful

7) Patient

8) Forgiving

✳

9) Amiable

10) Impartial

Personal Style of Behavior

1) Spontaneous truthfulness—irrespective of consequences

2) Dutiful out of love and respect

3) Outspoken when necessary

4) Having sense of propriety, modest

5) Simple, frank

6) Love for mental and physical cleanliness

7) Grateful toward benefactors

8) Contented

9) Sense of self-respect

Appendix B: Charts

_____'s Empathy Chart for the Week of_____

Names	Monday	Tuesday	Wednesday	Thursday	Friday

Instructions for this chart are on page 37. This chart can be increased on copier by 129% to full size.

_____'s Feelings Chart for the Week of_____

Times	Monday	Tuesday	Wednesday	Thursday	Friday

Instructions for this chart are on page 52. This chart can be increased on copier by 129% to full size.

Appendix B: Charts

✳

___'s Feelings Chart for the Week of ___

	Monday	Tuesday	Wednesday	Thursday	Friday
Happy #1					
Happy #2					
Bored					
Sad					

Monday ___

Tuesday ___

Wednesday ___

Thursday ___

Friday ___

Instructions for this chart are on page 53. This chart can be increased on copier by 129% to full size.

_____'s Will Power Chart for the Week of _____

	Monday	Tuesday	Wednesday	Thursday	Friday
One Thing at a Time					
Finishing a Project					
Something new					

Monday _____

Tuesday _____

Wednesday _____

Thursday _____

Friday _____

Instructions for this chart are on page 66. This chart can be increased on copier by 129% to full size.

✳ **Appendix B: Charts**

143

_____'s Meditation Chart for the Week of _____

	Monday	Tuesday	Wednesday	Thursday	Friday
Number of Breaths Counted					
Number of Mantra Recitations					
Level of Concentration*					

*Concentration

Level 1: Mind wanders away from point of concentration
Level 2: Mind wavers, but basically stays focused
Level 3: mind concentrates one-pointedly without interruption

Instructions for this chart are on page 115. This chart can be increased on copier by 129% to full size.

✳

Index

Other Recommended titles from Crystal Clarity Publishers

Education for Life
Preparing Children to Meet the Challenges
By J. Donald Walters

Here is a constructive alternative to modern education. The author stresses spiritual values and helping children grow toward full maturity learning not only facts, but also innovative principles for better living. This book is the basis for the Living Wisdom schools and the Education for Life Foundation, which trains teachers, parents and educators. Encouraging parents and educators to see children through their soul qualities, this unique system promises to be a much needed breath of fresh air.

Scary News
12 Ways to Raise Joyful Children When the Headlines Are Full of Fear
By Lorna Ann Knox

Scary News reassures parents that they can give their children the skills needed to cope with a complex and frightening world filled with war, terrorism, natural disasters, and economic uncertainty, while teaching them to be guided by love, not fear. A comforting and practical guide filled with realistic suggestions for protecting and nurturing a child's joyful inner spirit, each chapter outlines how to consciously decrease the power of fear and create a life experience of love, appreciation, beauty, and hope for the entire family. The author uses scientific research to explain why it is important to protect children from the frightening realities of today's headlines while encouraging parents that their intuition is their greatest asset.

I Came From Joy!
Spiritual Affirmations and Activities for Children
By Lorna Knox

This beautifully conceived, non-sectarian tool for developing a child's inner, spiritual life—ideal for parents, teachers, youth group leaders, and religious educators. Written for children age 5-11, but adaptable for all ages, *I Came From Joy!* offers fun and uplifting exercises that teach children 26 values including kindness, love, concentration, happiness, discrimination, sharing, patience, security, and how to be a success. This workbook includes full lesson plans, reproducible picture pages, guidance on how to teach spiritual values, and a list of recommended books and resources.

I Came From Joy!
Music to Make Your Heart Sing!
Sung by the Joy Singers
CD: 7-98499-50232-6

Featuring songs referenced in the book *I Came From Joy!*, this delightful recording can be used in conjunction with the book, or listened to by itself. This music will encourage happiness and self-worth in children throughout the pre-school and primary years.